John Squair, John Home Cameron

Exercises in French Prose

John Squair, John Home Cameron

Exercises in French Prose

ISBN/EAN: 9783337075651

Printed in Europe, USA, Canada, Australia, Japan

Cover: Foto ©Paul-Georg Meister /pixelio.de

More available books at **www.hansebooks.com**

The W. J. Gage Co.'s Educational Series.

EXERCISES
IN
FRENCH PROSE

BY

JOHN SQUAIR, B.A.,
Associate-Professor of French in University College, Toronto.

AND

JOHN HOME CAMERON, B.A.,
Lecturer in French in University College, T

TORONTO:
THE W. J. GAGE COMPANY (LT
1895.

Entered according to Act of Parliament of Canada, in the office of the Minister of Agriculture, by THE W. J. GAGE COMPANY Limited), in the year one thousand eight hundred and ninety-five.

PREFACE.

THE present volume has been constructed with the view of furnishing a few exercises which can be translated with considerable ease into French. Samples of the writings of the masters of English prose have been altogether avoided, for the reason that it is next to impossible to find extracts in the great authors which do not contain passages that are quite untranslatable. Many of the pieces have been made specially for the book, and in the case of those not made for it, all have been closely scanned, and in many cases reconstructed, so as to meet the desired end. If it be found by teachers that the book is too easy for any student, it is strongly recommended that such a student be troubled no longer with translation exercises, but that he be at once set to compose in French. Indeed even for those who are not far enough advanced to do such exercises as are contained in this book, there ought to be ample exercise in oral and written composition in addition to any translation that may be done from English into French. There can be little doubt that at present too much translation is being done in our language classes, and too little composition.

The book is divided into four parts. Part I. is made up of passages in French, which may be used as dictation exercises, and of passages in English, modelled on the French passages, to be turned into French. This is the simplest part of the book, and for advanced students will probably be of small utility. The other parts are each of about equal difficulty, so that the teacher is free to choose such pieces as have the most suitable subjects for the class of students he is dealing with. Part II. is composed of anecdotes and witticisms, and it is hoped that, besides its use in the matter of written exercises, it may afford materials to teachers in oral composition. Parts III. and IV. treat of French history, geography, etc., and it is believed that, in addition to being useful exercises in translation, they will convey such information to students as will make them take a greater interest in France and French institutions. It is of great importance that students of the French language should become as soon as possible interested in French things.

Explanatory notes have purposely been made as rare as possible. Any information not supplied in them which cannot be found in the vocabulary, or in the grammars in use in the schools, can be easily supplied by the teacher.

The vocabulary has been made with care. The definitions, although in the main of a general character, are yet often suited only to the cases arising in the text of the exercises. It is not claimed that where a phrase is translated, the rendering given is the best possible; it is simply one way,—that nearest to the English—of saying what the phrase would mean when expressed in fairly idiomatic French. With regard to proper names, only such are inserted as have a different orthography in French, or respecting which it was necessary to indicate the gender.

University College, Toronto,
January, 1895.

EXERCISES IN FRENCH PROSE.

PART I.—EXERCISES WITH MODELS.

I.

On parlait dans une société de l'Amérique. "C'est un charmant pays, dit un homme avec emphase.—Monsieur le connaît, à ce qu'il paraît, dit la maîtresse de la maison.—Parbleu! répond notre homme, si je le connais, j'ai un de mes frères qui a manqué d'y aller."

A man speaking of America in company said pompously that it was a charming country. The mistress of the house said to him, "It appears that you know the country." "Know it! My brothers were nearly going there!"

II.

Charles XII dictait une lettre à un de ses secrétaires. Une bombe tombe sur la tente et éclate près du secrétaire, qui s'arrête. "Qu'y a-t-il donc? lui dit le roi d'un air tranquille; pourquoi n'écrivez-vous pas?—Mais, sire, la bombe!—Eh! qu'a de commun la bombe avec la lettre que je vous dicte? Continuez."

As Charles XII. was dictating a letter to a secretary a bomb fell and burst near them. The secretary stopped, and the King asked him what[1] was the matter; and when he replied that it[2] was the bomb, the king told him to keep on, for the bomb had nothing to do with the letter he was writing.

III.

On présentait à Louis XIV un officier pour remplir une place. "Cet homme, dit le roi, est trop âgé.- Sire, reprit l'officier en habile courtisan, je n'ai que quatre ans de plus que votre majesté, et j'ai encore vingt-cinq ans à la servir." Le roi lui accorda ce qu'il demandait.

An officer having been presented to Louis XIV. for a certain position, the king said[3] the man was too old. But when the officer replied that he was only four years older than the king himself, and that he had still twenty-five years to serve his sovereign, the king granted him what he wished.

IV.

Madame de la Sablière logeait La Fontaine, qu'elle aimait, qu'elle estimait, et que sans cesse elle plaisantait. Un jour qu'elle avait fait maison nette en

---

[1] Note the difference in such expressions, according as they have the direct interrogative form or the indirect: *Je leur demande, "Qu' a-t-il?"* as compared with, *Je leur demande ce qu'il a.*

[2] Use *ce.*

[3] In such cases the conjunction *que* is never omitted in French.

congédiant tous ses domestiques, elle dit : "Je n'ai gardé avec moi que mes trois animaux : mon chat, mon chien, et mon La Fontaine."

Many anecdotes are told[1] of the poet La Fontaine; this is one of them. One of his friends, Madame de la Sablière, who loved[2] and esteemed him but who often made fun of him, said, after she had on one occasion dismissed all her servants, that she had kept only her three pets, her cat, her dog and her La Fontaine.

v.

Un aveugle, allant le soir chercher de l'eau à la fontaine, portait une cruche avec une chandelle allumée. "A quoi vous sert votre chandelle, lui dit un passant, puisque vous ne voyez goutte ?—C'est, répondit l'aveugle, pour avertir les étourdis comme toi de ne pas me heurter, et de ne pas casser ma cruche."

One evening a passer-by met a blind man who was going to the fountain for water, and who was carrying a lighted candle as well as his pitcher. When the passer-by asked him what use his candle was to him, he replied that it warned thoughtless fellows not to run against him and break his pitcher.

---

[1] Translate. "one tells."
[2] Do not omit the object.

VI.

Marivaux voyant un homme qui demandait l'aumône, et qui paraissait jouir d'une santé assez brillante, lui en fit l'observation. "Pourquoi ne travaillez-vous pas? Vous avez l'air frais et vigoureux.—Ah! monsieur, répondit le mendiant, si vous saviez comme je suis paresseux!—Tiens, dit Marivaux, voilà un écu pour ta franchise!"

Marivaux met one day a man asking for alms. Seeing that he was enjoying good health, Marivaux said to him that he seemed strong and asked him why he did not work. The beggar replied that if people knew how lazy he was, they[1] would have pity on him; whereupon Marivaux gave him a crown for his frankness.

VII.

Un vol avait été commis dans une petite paroisse. Le curé, à qui on avait fait des révélations, assembla ses paroissiens et leur dit: "Mes très chers frères, il y a un voleur parmi vous; comme vous accableriez le coupable de tout le poids de votre mépris, je me garderai bien de le nommer, mais voilà son chien qui dort tranquillement au pied de cette chaire de vérité."

The good priest of a parish where a theft had been committed, having called his parishioners together, said to them that since they would not fail to crush the thief with the full weight of their contempt, he

---

[1] Repeat the *on*.

would take good care not to mention his name. However, pointing to a dog sleeping at the foot of the pulpit, he said: "There's his dog."

VIII.

Un ambassadeur de France à la cour de Venise se plaignait, dans une audience, de ce que la république faisait féliciter le roi son maître sur un avantage considérable qu'il avait remporté sur l'Espagne avec qui il était en guerre, et qu'en même temps elle faisait témoigner au roi d'Espagne la part qu'elle prenait à sa perte. Le doge répondit à l'ambassadeur que cela ne devait point l'étonner, puisque la sérénissime république pratiquait en cela cette leçon de l'apôtre de se réjouir avec ceux qui sont dans la joie, et de s'affliger avec ceux qui sont dans l'affliction.

The king of France had won a considerable advantage over the king of Spain, and the court of Venice congratulated the one and expressed to the other the sympathy it felt in his loss. The French ambassador complained of this, but the doge replied that the Republic was only practising the lesson of the Apostle, who has taught us to rejoice with them that do rejoice and weep with them that weep.

IX.

Le cardinal de Retz disait un jour à Ménage : "Apprenez-moi un peu à me connaître en vers, afin que je puisse du moins juger de ceux qu'on m'apporte.

—Monsieur, lui répondit Ménage, ce serait une chose trop longue à vous apprendre; mais lorsqu'on vous en lira, dites toujours que cela ne vaut rien; vous ne courrez ainsi presque jamais le risque de vous tromper."

Cardinal de Retz desiring to be a good judge of verses so that he might be able to pronounce on those brought¹ to him, Ménage advised him when he read¹ any to say that they were worthless and that he would thus never run¹ the risk of being mistaken.

X.

Au milieu de la grande crise de la guerre de sept ans, un des soldats de Frédéric II déserte; il est pris et on le lui amène. "Pourquoi me quittais-tu? lui demande Frédéric.—Ma foi, sire, répond le déserteur, vos affaires sont si mauvaises que j'ai pensé qu'il fallait les abandonner.—Eh bien! reste encore jusqu'à demain, et si elles ne sont pas meilleures, nous déserterons ensemble."

During the Seven Years' War, one of Frederick's soldiers having deserted was caught and brought to the king. When the king asked him why he wished to desert, he replied that the king's cause was so bad that he was forced to abandon it. The king asked him to wait till the next day, saying that if matters were not better, he would then desert too.

---

¹ Use the conditional.

XI.

Roquelaure n'était pas beau. Il rencontre un jour un Auvergnat fort laid, qui avait des affaires à Versailles. Il le présente lui-même à Louis XIV, en lui disant qu'il avait les plus grandes obligations à ce gentilhomme. Le roi accorde la grâce qu'on lui demande, et s'informe du duc quelles sont les obligations qu'il a à cet homme. "Ah! sire, reprend Roquelaure, les plus grandes ; car, sans ce magot-là, je serais l'homme le plus laid de votre royaume."

Roquelaure, who was not very fine-looking, meeting one day at Versailles a very homely Auvergnat, presented him to the king, and asked some favor for him, saying that he was under great obligations to this man. When the king asked what the obligations were, Roquelaure replied that if it were not for the Auvergnat he would be the homeliest man in the kingdom.

XII.

Frédéric II, étant un jour à regarder par une fenêtre, s'aperçut qu'un de ses pages prenait une prise de tabac dans sa boîte, qui était sur la table. Il ne l'empêcha point ; mais se retournant après, il lui dit : "Cette tabatière est-elle de ton goût ?" Le page, fort embarrassé, garda le silence. Le roi répéta la question. Le page dit, en tremblant, qu'il la trouvait fort belle. "En ce cas, dit Frédéric, garde-la, parce qu'elle est trop petite pour deux."

One of the pages of Frederick II. was taking a pinch of snuff out of the king's snuff-box when the king noticed him, turned round, and asked him if he liked the snuff-box. The page at first was silent, but replied afterwards that he thought it very nice. Then the king told him to keep it, in that case, since it was too small for two.

XIII.

Un ecclésiastique, passant dans les rues de Paris, fut inondé d'eau bouillante par une fenêtre. Il s'essuya, se sécha du mieux qu'il put, et regagna sa maison d'un pas chancelant. Arrivé le visage gonflé et à moitié épilé, sa nièce et sa gouvernante jetaient les hauts cris; elles l'excitaient à la vengeance. "Mon Dieu! qu'avez-vous fait à ces misérables?—Je les ai remerciés.—Remerciés! eh! de quoi?—De ce qu'ils n'avaient pas jeté la marmite, car au lieu de m'échauder la tête ils me l'auraient cassée."

Some boiling water was thrown out of a window upon a priest who was going along the streets of Paris. Having dried himself as well as he could, he reached his house with a swollen and scalded face. When asked[1] what he had done to the wretches who had drenched him, he said he had thanked them for not having thrown the pot, which instead of scalding him would have broken his head.

XIV.

Un enfant s'était obstiné toute la matinée à ne pas vouloir dire *a*, la première lettre de son alphabet, et

---

[1] Translate, "when one asked him."

on l'avait fouetté pour son obstination. Un monsieur le trouve tout en pleurs, et on lui en dit la cause ; il appelle l'enfant, le prend sur ses genoux, et lui dit : "Mon petit ami, pourquoi n'avez-vous pas voulu dire *a*? Cela n'est pas bien difficile." L'enfant répond d'un ton chagrin : "C'est que je n'aurais pas plutôt dit *a*, qu'on me ferait dire *b*."

A child had been whipped for his obstinacy in not wishing to say *a*, the first letter of the alphabet. A gentleman who found him in tears called him to him, took him on his knee and asked him why he had been unwilling to say *a*. The child replied that if he had said *a*, they would have made him[1] say *b*.

XV.

Alphonse, roi d'Aragon, était venu voir les bijoux d'un joaillier avec plusieurs de ses courtisans. Il fut à peine sorti de la boutique, que le marchand courut après lui, pour se plaindre du vol qu'on lui avait fait d'un diamant de grand prix. Le roi rentra chez le marchand, et fit apporter un grand vase plein de son. Il ordonna que chacun de ses courtisans y mît la main fermée, et l'en retirât tout ouverte. Il commença le premier. Après que tout le monde y eut passé, il ordonna au joaillier de vider le vase sur la table. Le diamant s'y trouva.

A king and his courtiers came to see a jeweller's jewels. As soon as they had gone out of the shop, the

---

[1] Indirect object required.

jeweller discovered that he had lost a diamond, and he ran after them and complained of it to the king. They returned to the shop and had a vessel full of bran brought. The king ordered each of his courtiers to put his closed hand into it and to draw it out open. After all had done this, the jeweller, by the order of the king, emptied the vessel on the table and the diamond was there.

XVI.

Louis XIV parlait un jour du pouvoir que les rois ont sur leurs sujets ; le comte de Guiche osa prétendre que ce pouvoir avait des bornes ; mais le roi, n'en voulant admettre aucune, lui dit avec emportement : "Si je vous ordonnais de vous jeter dans la mer, vous devriez, sans hésiter, y sauter la tête la première." Le comte au lieu de répliquer, se retourna brusquement et prit le chemin de la porte. Le roi lui demanda avec étonnement où il allait. "Apprendre à nager, sire," lui répondit-il.

Whilst Louis XIV. was speaking of the power kings have over their subjects, one of his nobles asserted that there were limits to this power. The king refused to admit it, and replied that, if he ordered one of his subjects to jump into the sea head first, he ought to obey. The count made no reply, but turning round quickly, made for the door. When the king asked him where he was going, he said, "I am off to learn to swim, your Majesty."

XVII.

Un Arabe, égaré dans le désert, n'avait pas mangé depuis deux jours et se voyait réduit à mourir de faim. En passant près d'un de ces puits où les caravanes viennent abreuver leurs chameux, il voit sur le sable un petit sac de cuir. Il le ramasse, il le tâte : "Allah soit béni! dit-il ; ce sont, je crois, des dattes ou des noisettes." Plein de cette douce espérance, il se hâta d'ouvrir le sac ; mais à la vue de ce qu'il contenait : "Hélas! s'écria-t-il douloureusement, je croyais que c'était au moins des noisettes, et ce ne sont que des perles."

An Arab had lost his way in the desert, and had been two days without food. At last he saw a little leathern bag on the sand near a well where people watered their camels. He hastened to pick it up, thinking that it contained something to eat, probably dates or nuts. But the poor man's hope was painfully deceived when he saw that he had found nothing but pearls.

XVIII.

On sait que Beaumarchais était le fils d'un horloger. Un homme de la cour le voyant passer avec un très bel habit dans la galerie de Versailles, s'approcha de lui, et lui dit : "Parbleu, monsieur de Beaumarchais, je vous rencontre à propos. Ma montre est dérangée ; faites-moi le plaisir d'y voir.—Volontiers, monsieur le marquis ; mais je vous préviens que je suis fort maladroit.—Pure modestie, monsieur; voyez-y, je vous prie." Beaumarchais prend la montre et la laisse tomber sur le pavé. "Mille excuses, monsieur le marquis; je vous avais bien dit que je ne suis pas adroit."

Beaumarchais the writer of the 18th century was the son of a watchmaker. One day as he was walking in the gallery at Versailles dressed in a fine coat, a man of the court saw him, and, wishing to insult him, said that their meeting was very opportune, since his watch was out of order, and asked Beaumarchais to take a look at it. The man of letters warned the nobleman that he was very clumsy, but the latter insisted. Beaumarchais then took the watch and let it fall on the floor, saying, "Did I not tell you that I was clumsy?"

XIX.

Un certain Parmenon imitait parfaitement le grognement du porc. Ses camarades, jaloux de la réputation qu'il s'était acquise par son talent, tâchaient de l'imiter, mais les spectateurs prévenus disaient toujours: "Cela est bien; mais qu'est-ce en comparaison du porc de Parmenon!" Un de ses rivaux prit un jour sous sa robe un jeune porc qu'il fit grogner. Les spectateurs, après avoir entendu ce cri naturel, dirent encore: "Qu'est-ce que cela auprès du porc de Parmenon!" Alors il lâcha son porc au milieu de l'assemblée, et les convainquit par là que c'était la prévention, et non la vérité qui dictait leur jugement.

One of the comrades of Parmenon being jealous of the reputation the latter had acquired in[1] imitating the grunting of a pig, took one day under his cloak a real young pig and made it grunt. The spectators, prejudiced in favor of Parmenon, said, as they always did, that it was nothing in comparison with his pig. Whereupon the rival let his pig loose among them, and they were convinced that it was prejudice which had always inspired their opinion.

XX.

Le feu roi de Prusse avait un aide de camp qui avait peu de fortune, et vivait dans la gêne; il lui envoie un petit portefeuille, en forme de livre, où il avait placé 500 thalers. Quelque temps après il rencontre l'officier. "Eh bien, lui dit-il, comment avez-vous trouvé l'ouvrage que je vous ai adressé?—Parfait, sire, répond le colonel, et même tellement intéressant que j'en attends le second volume avec impatience." Le roi sourit; et, quand vint la fête de l'officier, il lui fit passer un nouveau portefeuille absolument semblable au premier, avec ces mots en tête du livre: "Cette œuvre[2] n'a que deux volumes."

The king of Prussia had sent to one of his *aides-de-camp*, who was in straitened circumstances, a little pocket-book in the form of a book, in which were 500 thalers. A few days after, he met the officer and

---

[1] Use à with the infinitive.
[2] This use of œuvre is uncommon. When referring to books, it is generally used in the plural to indicate the collective productions of an author: *Les œuvres complètes de Molière, Racine,* etc.

asked him how he liked the work which had been sent to him. The officer replied that he liked it very much and was waiting impatiently for the second volume. The king said nothing, but on the officer's birth-day he sent him a second pocket-book like the first, with these words for a heading : "This work has only two volumes."

XXI.

Le Sage, l'auteur de *Gil Blas*, avant de faire jouer son *Turcaret*, avait promis à la duchesse de Bouillon d'aller lui lire sa pièce ; on comptait que la lecture s'en ferait avant le dîner, mais quelques affaires retinrent l'auteur, et il arriva tard. La duchesse de Bouillon le reçut d'un air d'impatience et avec une hauteur outrageante. "Vous m'avez fait perdre une heure à vous attendre, lui dit-elle.—Eh bien, madame, reprit froidement Le Sage, je vais vous en faire gagner deux." Il fit sa révérence et sortit.

Le Sage, the great French author, promised a certain duchess to read to her his play *Turcaret*, before having it played. The duchess expected that it would be read before dinner, but Le Sage, being detained by some business, arrived late, and she received him with insulting haughtiness, saying to him that he had made her[1] lose an hour in waiting for him. Le Sage replied that if he had caused her to lose an hour, he would now cause her to gain two, and he made his bow and departed.

---

[1] See page 9, note 1.

XXII.

Henri IV, égaré dans une forêt, rencontre un paysan, qu'il prie de lui servir de guide. Chemin faisant, le paysan dit au prince : "Monsieur, vous êtes sûrement un des premiers officiers du roi ; je ne l'ai jamais vu. Ne pourrais-je pas, par votre bonne grâce, le voir aujourd'hui ?—Volontiers ! dit Henri ; lorsque nous serons arrivés, tu n'auras qu'à te tenir à côté de moi, et parmi tous ceux qui approcheront tu remarqueras celui qui aura le chapeau sur la tête ; ce sera le roi." Arrivé au lieu du rendez-vous, les courtisans que l'absence du roi avait mis dans l'inquiétude, s'empressèrent de l'aborder, le chapeau à la main. Henri, que le paysan continuait d'accompagner, le chapeau sur la tête, se retournant vers cet homme, lui dit : "Eh bien ! vois-tu qui est-ce qui est le roi ?—Ma foi, monsieur, dit le paysan, c'est vous ou moi."

Henry IV. lost himself one day in a forest, and, having met a peasant, he asked him to serve him as guide. As they went along, the peasant said that he had never seen the king, and asked the stranger if he could not see him on this occasion. Henry replied that when they should arrive at the meeting place, he would notice the one who had[1] a hat on his head, and that would be the king. When they arrived, the courtiers approached the king with their hats in their hands. Henry then turned round to the peasant and asked whether he saw which was the king, and the peasant answered : "It must be either you or I."

[1] Translate by the conditional.

XXIII.

Dix ans après (1534), Le Breton Jacques Cartier, de Saint-Malo, commissionné par le roi sur la proposition de l'amiral Chabot de Brion, s'assura que Terre-Neuve était une île, pénétra dans le vaste golfe que barre cette grande île et reconnut l'embouchure du Saint-Laurent : il remonta ce fleuve immense l'année suivante jusqu'au lieu où plus tard fut bâti Québec et découvrit le Canada. Le nom de Nouvelle-France fut imposé à tout le nord de l'Amérique. En 1540, Roberval, gentilhomme picard, fut nommé par François Ier vice-roi du Canada et partit avec une escadre de cinq navires que Cartier commandait sous ses ordres : la colonie fut installée au Cap-Breton ; la rigueur du climat, si différent des magnifiques régions conquises par les Espagnols, l'insuffisance des ressources, l'imprévoyance et la négligence du gouvernement royal firent échouer, au bout de quelques années, ce premier essai de colonisation, qu'on ne renouvela plus jusqu'au règne de Henri IV ; mais les marins normands, bretons et rochelois continuèrent la pêche de la morue et le commerce des pelleteries avec les peuples du Canada.

In 1534 Jacques Cartier, who had been commissioned by the king, discovered the Island of Newfoundland, and, having entered into a great gulf, reconnoitred the mouth of the St. Lawrence. In the following year he ascended this great river and discovered the spot on which Quebec was afterwards built. In 1540 the king appointed Roberval, a nobleman of Picardy, viceroy of New France, and he and Cartier departed with a squadron of five ships. The first attempt at colonisation was made at Cape Breton, but it failed after a few years on account of the severity of the climate and the negligence of the king's government; it was only in the reign of Henry IV. that the attempt was renewed. But codfishing and the fur trade were continued by sailors from Normandy, Brittany and La Rochelle.

XXIV.

Il n'est nulle part un pays arrosé par de plus belles et de plus grandes rivières que le Canada, que traverse le fleuve Saint-Laurent dans toute l'étendue de son cours : le fleuve Saint-Laurent, navigable pour les plus grands vaisseaux jusqu'à Québec, distance de 150 lieues de son embouchure, navigable pour les navires de 600 tonneaux de port jusqu'à Montréal, soixante autres lieues, et que sillonnent partout des vapeurs et des bâtiments à voiles des plus grandes dimensions. Le flux de la mer se fait sentir jusqu'à Trois-Rivières à trente lieues au-dessus de Québec : dans le port de Québec les marées s'élèvent à un maximum de vingt pieds, et ont une moyenne élévation de douze pieds, car de ce port vers le golfe le grand fleuve affecte toutes les allures de la mer.

(Written in 1855.)

There are nowhere larger rivers than those which water Canada, the chief of which is the St. Lawrence, which flows through the country throughout its whole course. The St. Lawrence is ploughed by the largest steamers and sailing vessels as far as Montreal, a distance of more than 200 leagues from its mouth. At

Quebec, situated 150 leagues from the gulf, the great river behaves quite like the sea. The tide rises sometimes to a height of twenty feet, and has an average height of twelve feet. The tide is felt even as far as Three Rivers, thirty leagues above Quebec.

XXV.

La monarchie des Valois ne se fit pas de telles destinées. Elle ne sut pas se rendre indépendante. Elle ne se fit pas protestante. Elle ne fut pas tout à fait ni constamment romaine et ultramontaine. Elle flotta d'une demi-tolérance à des persécutions atroces et devint le dernier des gouvernements de la chrétienté; car les autres avaient une politique et elle n'en eut pas. Au lieu d'empêcher les guerres de religion, elle les attira chez nous, fit de la France non l'arbitre, mais la proie de l'Europe, et de notre sol l'affreux champ de bataille des sectes et des nations. La dynastie périt étouffée dans le sang et dans la boue, et la France eût péri avec elle, si la Providence ne nous eût envoyé un guerrier et un politique de premier ordre. Henri IV nous sauva, digne assurément d'une immortelle mémoire.

The Valois dynasty became the weakest of the governments of Europe, because it wavered between persecutions and tolerance, because it did not become Protestant, and was not altogether Catholic. It was not able to make itself independent. It had no policy whilst the other nations of Christendom had. Instead of making France the arbiter of Europe, the dynasty made it the prey of other nations. It was unable to hinder religious wars, and France became the battlefield of the sects. But Henry IV. saved the nation, and his name is worthy of immortal memory. If this great warrior and statesman had not been sent by Providence, France would have perished, just as the dynasty itself perished, in blood and dishonor.

XXVI.

Devant ces faits une conviction s'impose. Les remèdes qui ont été impuissants dans le passé le seront encore de nos jours : celui qui a triomphé jadis de l'anarchisme doit en triompher encore une fois. On ne prétend pas que le péril actuel ne sera conjuré que par un mouvement en tout analogue à celui du XVIe siècle, c'est-à-dire par une expansion nouvelle du protestantisme. On affirme seulement que la force qui eut alors raison du Libre Esprit doit manifester de nouveau sa vertu. Quelque forme qu'il revête, il nous faut pour nous sauver un réveil du sens moral. La guillotine, les fusillades, la déportation supprimeront des anarchistes ; elles pourront ramener le mal à des proportions rassurantes pour les esprits superficiels : elles laisseront subsister un levain qui n'attendra pour s'agiter que des circonstances plus favorables. Les améliorations sociales elles-mêmes, jusqu'aux plus radicales et aux plus heureuses, seront insuffisantes à diminuer la somme de haine dans le monde, si les appétits ne sont refrénés par une force intime. La tâche actuelle, c'est le rappel de la justice, la restauration de la loi intérieure qui nous libère de tous les pouvoirs arbitraires et nous contraint souvent de marcher contre nos propres désirs ; c'est en un mot, le redressement de la conscience morale.

In presence of these facts one conviction forces itself upon us. The remedy which in the 16th century triumphed over anarchism will triumph over it once again. We do not claim that a new expansion of Protestantism is the only thing which can drive away the present peril, we merely affirm that an awakening of the moral sense similar to that which got the better of the "Free Spirit" must manifest itself again. The guillotine will do away with some anarchists, no doubt; it may lessen[1] the evil to a certain extent: but it will allow a leaven to remain which will work as soon as the conditions are favorable. But if our appetites are not restrained by an inward law, even the most radical and successful social improvements will not be able to diminish the sum of hatred in the world. What we need to save us is a hidden force which will constrain us to go against our desires, which will free us from all arbitrary powers; in a word, we need the rectification of the moral conscience.

XXVII.

Les États-Unis semblaient, naguère encore, devoir échapper aux conflits qui troublent en Europe le domaine de l'industrie. Suivant l'expression consacrée, quoique un peu démodée, la démocratie y coule à pleins bords. La nation se gouverne elle-même et le misérable nègre des plantations du Sud possède des droits politiques égaux à ceux du millionnaire.

---

[1] Use *amoindrir*.

propriétaire d'une mine à *bonanza*, roi du pétrole ou des chemins de fer. Le domaine public est à peine entamé ; des millions d'hectares sont à la disposition des travailleurs économes, qui peuvent obtenir une concession de bonne terre et un *homestead*, moyennant une faible avance de capital. Comment donc se fait-il que, dans cette contrée nouvelle et privilégiée, la lutte du capital et du travail ait pris, en quelques années, des proportions qu'elle n'a pas acquises en un demi-siècle, dans nos vieilles sociétés, et qu'elle s'y déploie avec une violence sauvage ? Ce phénomène déplorable, nos socialistes n'ont pas manqué de l'attribuer au "laisser faire." On approcherait davantage de la vérité, en l'attribuant au système de protection qui a surexcité artificiellement aux États-Unis le développement de l'industrie manufacturière.

The conflicts between labor and capital which have disturbed the peace of Europe, seemed fated not to afflict the United States. In that country democracy flows in a full stream. The railway king or the oil king has not greater political rights than the poor negro of the South. With a little capital, the industrious may obtain a grant of good land amongst the millions of acres which are at their disposal. But in this privileged country the struggle between labor and capital manifests itself with great violence, and has assumed proportions which it has not acquired even in Europe. How is this ? The socialists attribute this sad phenomenon to the system of "laisser faire" which exists. But perhaps we should be nearer the truth if we attributed it to the system of protection, which has over-excited the development of manufacturing industry.

XXVIII.

Les chefs des royaumes et des républiques ont mis dans leurs livres que le droit des gens est le droit de guerre. Et ils ont glorifié la violence. Et ils rendent des honneurs aux conquérants, et ils élèvent sur les places publiques des statues à l'homme et au cheval victorieux. Mais le droit n'est pas de tuer : c'est pourquoi le juste ne tirera pas de l'urne son numéro à la conscription. Le droit n'est pas de nourrir la folie et les crimes du prince qui est élevé sur le royaume ou sur la république : et c'est pourquoi le juste ne paiera pas l'impôt ; et il ne donnera point d'argent aux publicains. Il jouira en paix du fruit de son travail, et il fera du pain avec le blé qu'il a semé, et il mangera les fruits des arbres qu'il a taillés.

The heads of kingdoms glorify violence in rendering honors to the conqueror and in raising statues to the victorious ; they have said that the right of nations is the right to kill. But a day will come when the just man will no longer draw his number to be a soldier, when he will no longer pay taxes, nor give his money to the tax-gatherer to support the crimes of princes. The poor will enjoy the fruit of their labor ; they will eat the bread made of the wheat they have sown and the fruits of the trees they have trimmed.

PART II.—ANECDOTES AND WITTICISMS.

I.

A[1] friend of an artist was endeavoring to persuade him not to devote so much time to his works.—"You don't know, then," said the painter, "that I have a master very difficult to please."—"Who is he?"— "Myself."

II.

A regular physician being sent for by a quack, expressed his surprise at being called in for an ailment apparently so trifling.—"Not so trifling," replied the quack, "for to tell you the truth, I have, by mistake, swallowed some of my own pills."

III.

A certain dramatic translator introducing a well-known comedian to Madame Vestris, said : "Madam, this is Mr. B., who is not such a fool as he looks."— "True, madam," said the comedian, "and that is the great difference between me and my friend."

IV.

A conceited young man asked Foote what apology he should make for not being one of a party, the day

---
[1] Translate, "the."

before, to which he had been invited.—"Oh, my dear sir," replied the wit, "say nothing about it, you were not missed[1]."

V.

Merchant: "Can you manage to make yourself understood when French and Spanish customers come to the office?"

Would-be Clerk: "Certainly, if they know how to talk English."

VI.

An ass complained to Æsop that the fabulist did not make him talk sensibly in his fables.—"Why, my dear friend," said Æsop laughing, "if I did that, I should be the ass and you the fabulist."

VII.

A man asked his friend why he had married so small a wife.—"Why," said the other, "I thought you knew that of all evils we should choose the least."

VIII.

Some one said of a slanderer, who always took undue advantage of the hospitality of those who had once given him an invitation, that he never opened his mouth but at the expense of his friends.

---

[1] Translate, "your absence was not noticed."

IX.

Some one once asked a lunatic, confined in an asylum, how he came there, and he answered: "By a dispute. People said I was mad, and I said they were mad, and they carried it against me."

X.

On board a ship that was just about to weigh anchor, an Irishman was ordered by one of the officers to go below and fetch a jug of water. The man hesitated, saying that as the vessel was just going to sail, he was afraid he should be left behind.

XI.

Vivier to his concierge: "Just try and find out how much they pay the dog on the first floor for barking like that all night. And you will offer him double, from me, to keep quiet."

XII.

A bohemian enters the shop of a fashionable tailor and asks the price of a pair of trousers.—"Sixty francs," replies the tailor. "By the by," he adds, "how do you want the pockets?"—"I don't want any," says the other, "I shan't have any more need of them when I have[1] paid you for my trousers."

---

[1] Use the future.

XIII.

Little Toto has several compliments to write for New Year's Day, and he asks his mother how he is to go about it.—"The best way," says his mother, "is to write as one speaks."—"Yes," says Toto, "but then, when you speak through your nose?"

XIV.

Here is a conundrum which has puzzled a good many people: There were once two blind beggars. And the two blind beggars had a brother. Then the brother died. Now the deceased never had any brothers. What relationship existed between the two blind beggars and the deceased?

They were his two sisters, to be sure.

XV.

"Francis, what has become of the letter that was on this table?" asked a captain of his servant.—"I have posted it, captain."—"But there was no address on it."—"Oh!" replied Francis, knowingly, "I noticed that quite well, but I thought you didn't want people to know whom you were writing to."

XVI.

A magistrate was doubtful whether a little boy who was presented as a witness understood the meaning of an oath. He therefore began by asking him a simple question : "My boy, can you repeat the Lord's Prayer?"—"Yes, sir," was the quick reply; "can you?"[1]

XVII.

Falconet, a celebrated physician, was one day called to see a lady who fancied she was ill. He questioned her; she admitted to him that she ate, drank and slept well, and that she had all the marks of perfect health.[2] —"Well," said the doctor to her, "leave it to me, I'll give you a remedy that will relieve you of all that."

XVIII.

A father on receiving his son's school-report says severely to the boy: "My son, this is disgraceful. Your report shows that you are the last boy in a class of twenty-two."

Henry: "It might have been worse, father."

Father: "I don't see how."

Henry: "There might have been more boys in the class."

XIX.

When the learned Dr. Johnson was courting the lady who later became his wife, he told her he was of lowly origin, possessed no means at all, and that an uncle of his had been hanged. The lady answered

---

[1] Translate, "and you?" or "can you say it yourself."
[2] Translate, "a perfect health."

that her means were not any greater than his own, and that, though hitherto none of her relatives had been hanged, she had more than twenty who richly deserved it. As is well known, the marriage took place.

XX.

A drunken fellow, in order to provide himself with drink, sold all his furniture except his feather bed. At last, in a moment of extreme thirst, he made away with the bed too. When some of his friends took him to task for it, he said: "Why, I am very well, thank Heaven, and why then should I keep my bed?"

XXI.

An ass had the presumption to run a race with a hunting-horse. The contest was so ridiculous that everybody made fun of the ass. But he had lost none of his self-sufficiency and said coolly, as soon as he recovered his breath: "I see now quite well why I have been beaten. Some months ago I ran a thorn into my foot, and it pains me yet."

XXII.

When the celebrated Beau Nash was ill, Dr. Cheyne wrote a prescription for him. The next day, when the doctor came, he asked his patient if he had followed his prescription. "No, truly, doctor," said Nash; "if I had, I should have broken my neck, for I threw it out of the second story window."

XXIII.

It is easy to laugh at a foreigner's mistakes. But was French ever worse murdered than on the evening when a passenger on one of the Atlantic steamers was heard telling a French lady that her berth was ready, in these words: "Madame votre naissance est arrangée?"

XXIV.

It is half-past twelve at night. The gas is out. Some one rings. The concierge, after pulling the cord, cries out: "Is that you from the fifth? You ought to shut the door properly when you come in." —"Why, I *have* shut your door."[1] —"Shut it harder, that I may know; but do it so as not to waken my wife."

XXV.

Malherbe was once dining with the Archbishop of Rouen, who was famous for his dull sermons. No sooner was dinner over than Malherbe fell asleep. The prelate awoke him and invited him to go and hear him preach. "I beseech your grace to excuse me," said the poet, "I can sleep extremely well where I am."

XXVI.

The wife of an Irish gentleman being taken ill, the husband ordered a servant to get a horse ready to go

---

[1] Translate, "I have shut it, your door."

to the next town for the doctor. When at last the horse was ready and the letter written, the lady felt better, on which her husband added the following postscript and sent off the messenger: "My wife being recovered, you need not come."

XXVII.

A gentleman in Ireland having built a large house, was at a loss what to do with the rubbish. His steward advised him to have a pit dug, large enough to contain it. "And what shall I do," said the gentleman, "with the earth which comes out of the pit?" To which the steward replied: "Have the pit made large enough to hold all."

XXVIII.

Raphael once painted a picture in which he introduced some of the apostles. Two cardinals found fault with the painting, because the faces of Saint Peter and Saint Paul were too red. "Be not astonished at that, my Lords," said the painter. "I have painted them as they are in heaven. They are blushing with shame to see the Church so badly governed."

XXIX.

Lord Chesterfield became at last so infirm that, whenever he went out in his carriage, the horses were led at a walk. One morning, when he was out driving in this quiet way, he met an acquaintance, who congratulated him on being able to leave his room. "I thank you kindly, sir," said the Earl; "but I come out, not so much[1] to take the air as for the purpose of rehearsing my funeral."

XXX.

An Irishman comparing his watch with the clock of St. Paul's cathedral, burst into a fit of laughter. When some one asked him why he was laughing, he answered: "And how can I help it? My little watch here, that was made by Paddy O'Flaherty, on Ormond Quay, and cost me five guineas, has beat your big London clock there a whole hour and a quarter since yesterday."

XXXI.

It is said that, when Dr. Johnson was in Scotland, he was taken to see a very ancient and high castle, from which one could see[2] a great distance. After much effort, the big Doctor reached the highest point in the castle. Then his guide turned to him and said in a tone of triumph: "Well, sir, what do you think of this prospect?"—"It is the finest in all Scotland," replied the great man; "for I can here see the road to England."

---

[1] Translate, "less."
[2] In such phrases, "could" followed by the infinitive, is often rendered by the simple imperfect.

XXXII.

A fly had placed herself upon the horn of a bull. "I ask your pardon," said she to him, "for the liberty I have taken; but if I weigh too heavily upon your head, you have only to say so, and I will fly away." —"Who is speaking to me up there?" demanded the bull with[1] a terrible voice; and when he saw who it was, "Oh! my lady Fly, is it you?" said he. "Don't be uneasy, I beseech you. I did not notice you when you settled on my head, and I shall certainly not miss you when you think fit to fly away."

XXXIII.

Rossini and a friend of his went to dine with a rich lady, who, although she wished to be thought generous, was really avaricious. The dinner was most wretched. As the guests were departing, the lady thanked the great musician for his kindness in accepting her invitation, saying: "I should be very much pleased, maestro, if before you leave Paris, you would do me the honor of dining with me a second time."—"Very gladly," replied Rossini, "and I shall do so at once, if you wish it."

XXXIV.

The vicar of a village church in England was going home after the service one Sunday, when one of his flock, a rich farmer, said to him: "Well,

---

[1] Use *de*.

parson, you are getting on pretty well now; but why don't you give us now and then a scrap of Latin?"— "Why," said the vicar, "if I had thought you wanted it, I should have had no objection. But I am afraid you would not understand it."—"That," said the farmer, "is nothing to you; as we pay for the best, we ought to have the best."

XXXV.

A lawyer who was very little, but also very learned and witty, had to appear one day as a witness before a court. Another lawyer who, as it happened, was of quite gigantic size, asked him what he was, and, after he had received an answer, cried out: "What! You a lawyer! Why, I could put you into my pocket."—"That may be," retorted the little man; "but if you did, you would have more jurisprudence in your pocket than in your head."

XXXVI.

Two friends met one day on the street. "Well!" said the one, "how goes it? What have you been doing lately?"—"Oh," said the other, "I have been rowing a good deal. The other day my man Pat and I rowed to H. Then we undressed and had a bath in the lake. When we were about half-dressed, a storm came up suddenly, and Pat immediately undressed again and sprang into the water. I asked him why."—"I don't want to get wet," was his answer.

XXXVII.

Once there was a brave little man who thought it was his duty to kill a big ogre. We don't know what the dispute was, but you may be sure the ogre was doing a good deal of harm, as he always does in the fairy tales. Well, the little man wished to get rid of the ogre, and he went about it in this way. He made a deep hole in the ground, and covered it so cleverly that the ogre did not know there was a hole there. Naturally, the ogre, in running after the little man, stepped on the branches which covered the hole, and fell in. You can imagine the sequel.

XXXVIII.

A certain man had much more riches than brains, and took great pleasure in making a display of his wealth. One day he had an old Irishman working[1] for him, and went to oversee the work. He looked a moment at Denis working hard, and said: "Well, Denis, it's good to be rich, isn't it."—"Yes, sir," said Denis, who had the wit of his nation.—"I am rich, very rich, Denis."—"Yes, sir."—"I own lands, and houses, and bonds, and stocks, and railways, and . . . and . . . and . . ."—"Yes, sir," said Denis, digging away.—"And what is it, Denis, that I haven't got?"—"Not a bit of sense, sir," said Denis, as he picked up his wheelbarrow and trundled it off full of earth.

---

[1] Translate, "who was working."

XXXIX.

Before the new buildings of the University of Jena were erected, the professors used to give their lectures in various public halls, here and there through the town. In the middle of one of these halls, where the professor of theology used to lecture, there was a large pillar. At the end of the term, when the students asked the professor for their certificates of attendance, the latter replied to one of the young men: "But, my dear sir, I never saw you during the whole year!"—"Oh, sir, I was always seated behind the pillar."—"That is very strange!" was the reply, "you are the seventh student who professes to have sat regularly behind the pillar."

XL.

A story is told of Malherbe the poet, that one day he was invited to dine with the Abbé Desportes. On arriving at the house of the Abbé, he found that the soup had already been served, and he desired very much to eat his before it should become cold. But the Abbé, who was also a poet, had composed some verses of which he was very proud. In his impatience to show them to Malherbe, the good Abbé could not wait till the former had eaten his soup, but was about to run to his cabinet for them, when Malherbe said it was not worth the while, for he had already seen the verses, and he could assure his friend, the Abbé, that his soup was better than his poetry. It is said that the Abbé was not pleased with this manner of praising his soup.

XLI.

When Sheridan's play, "The School for Scandal," was first played, Cumberland's children persuaded their father to take them to see it. They had a stage-box, and their father sat behind them. Every time the children laughed at what was going on on the stage, he pinched them and said: "What are you laughing at, my dear little folks? You should not laugh, my little dears; there is nothing to laugh at;" and then, in an under-tone: "Keep still, you little dunces."

When Sheridan heard of this, long afterwards, he said: "It was very ungrateful in Cumberland to have been displeased with his poor children for laughing at my comedy; for I went the other night to see his tragedy, and laughed at it from beginning to end."

XLII.

The coach had come to a hill. The road was bad and the weather was hot. The six horses were pulling hard. All the travellers had got out and were walking behind the coach. A fly suddenly arrives, flies straight at the horses, buzzes about their ears, stings them and imagines that she is making things go. She sits on the pole, then on the coachman's nose, and flies everywhere. As soon as the coach advances, she attributes to herself all the glory, and when it stops, she complains that no one is working except her. At last, after great efforts, the coach reaches the top of the hill. "Now," says the fly, "let us take breath. I have worked so hard that you are up. You won't need me any longer, I hope. But I want my reward before I leave you."

The moral of the fable is not hard to find.

XLIII.

A wolf had carried off a lamb. As he was running through the wood, he met a fox who had seized a hen and was carrying it to his hole. "Friend," said the wolf, "where are you running so fast? Don't be in such a hurry; come and join your breakfast to mine, and we shall feast together to-day." The fox, on this occasion, was foolish enough to consent, and carried his hen to the wolf. The latter naturally found it too delicate a morsel for a fox, and devoured it himself. The poor fox lost his breakfast, and had to content himself with trotting meekly behind the wolf, fearing that he might be obliged to keep the hen company, if he complained.

XLIV.

A wolf was about to die, and was thinking of his long and wicked life. "I have done wrong sometimes," said he, "but there are many people in the world who are worse than I am. I have often rendered important services to others. I recollect that one day a poor little lamb passed by my house. I wished very much to kill it and eat it, but I had pity on its weakness. Precisely at that moment I heard the insulting words of a sheep. I had nothing to fear, for the dogs were sleeping peacefully."—"I can bear witness to all the facts which you have related," said a fox, who was present and who was caring for him in his last illness, "for it was at the time when you came very near being strangled by that bone from which the crane had the kindness to deliver you."

XLV.

A friend of mine told me this story the other day. In a certain battle, a soldier had his leg carried off by a cannon-ball. An Irishman was ordered to carry him to the ambulance-waggon. He took up the wounded man and made his way towards the place indicated. On the way, however, a second ball carried off the man's head. But the Irishman was so busy that he did not notice it. When he reached the ambulance, the surgeon said sharply: "Why have you brought that man here? Don't you see his head is gone?"

The Irishman laid his burden on the ground, and, after looking at it for a moment, said in a tone of vexation: "Well, the rascal told me just now it was his leg; but I ought to have suspected him. He has always been a dreadful liar."

XLVI.

Frederick the Great had in his body-guard a corporal who wore a watch-guard. The king said to him one day, to tease him: "By the by, corporal, you must have been very saving to buy a watch. It is six o'clock by mine; what time is it by yours?" The soldier, guessing the king's intention, at once drew the chain from his fob, showing a musket-bullet attached to the end, instead of a watch, and answered: "My watch marks neither five o'clock nor six; but it tells me every moment that it is my duty to die for your Majesty."—"Here, my friend," said the king, giving the corporal his own watch, "take this watch, that you may be able to tell the time also."

XLVII.

An octogenarian was planting trees. Three young men passed by. "The man must be mad," said one.—"That's evident; he will never live to gather the fruit of his labor," said another.—"My good man," cried the third, "it is high time you were thinking of death. Leave that work to us who have life before us."—"Ah! my children," said the old man kindly, "who knows which of us shall outlive the rest? Meantime, I hope you will not forbid me to enjoy the pleasure of working for those who are coming after me. That is a fruit I am already enjoying to-day, and I may continue to do so to-morrow and longer. Indeed, I may yet see the sun rise upon your graves."

He was right. One of the young men was drowned going to America. Another fell in war. The third was killed by a fall from a tree he himself was going to graft. And the old man lived to weep for them all.

XLVIII.

Henry VIII. appointed Sir Thomas More to carry to Francis I. of France an expression of his displeasure. Sir Thomas told him that he feared, if he carried such a message to so violent a king as Francis, it[1] might cost him his head.—"Have no fear," said the king, "if Francis should cut off your head, I would make every Frenchman now in London a head shorter."—"I am obliged to your Majesty," said Sir Thomas, "but I much fear that none of their heads would fit my shoulders."

XLIX.

During a war in Italy, a gentleman who was returning home late at night was robbed of his cloak by some soldiers. He complained to the celebrated chief of the brigands, Facino Cane, telling him that some of his men had taken his cloak, and saying he hoped the general would not leave them unpunished. Facino, looking at the gentleman, asked him how he was dressed when he lost his cloak.—"Just as I am at present," replied he.—"Then," said the chief, "it

---

[1] Translate, "that."

was[1] not my men who robbed you, for I am sure there is not one of them who would have left you so good a coat as that you wear now."

L.

A sailor on board of a war-ship had the misfortune to let a silver tea-pot fall into the sea. Full of apprehension he went to the cabin of the captain, and said to him : "Captain[2], can one say of a thing that it is lost, if one knows where it is?"—"If the place where it is, is known," replied the captain, "certainly not."—"In that case, captain, I have nothing to fear on account of your tea-pot," said the sailor, "because I know that it is at the bottom of the sea."

LI.

The emperor Joseph of Austria arrived one day before his retinue at a small town, and went to lodge at an inn. The landlady, who was somewhat inquisitive, asked him whether he belonged to the retinue of the emperor, to which the prince replied that he did not. But the good woman was little satisfied with so laconic an answer. Hence she sought to enter his apartment under some pretext to find out who he really was. She did this, and, seeing that he was shaving himself, she asked him if he held any office about his majesty. "Yes, certainly," replied the monarch, "I shave him sometimes."

---

[1] Use the present.
[2] Insert, "my."

LII.

All the animals, except the fox, had gone to visit a sick lion, to condole with him about his sickness. A wolf called the attention of the lion to the absence of the fox. The lion swore he would avenge himself. The cunning fox knew what fate awaited him, and ran to the lion, to whom he spoke thus : "O magnanimous king, behold before you your most faithful subject. Whilst all these animals were speaking to you here words of condolence, more or less sincere, I was elsewhere, all intent on finding a remedy for your sickness. It is this : Let them take the skin still warm, of a wolf flayed alive and wrap the august patient in it." So it was done.

LIII.

The well-known English poet Gray had a great dread of fire and had always a rope-ladder in his sleeping-room. Some of his friends knew this, and determined to play him a trick, in order to cure him of his fear. One cold winter night, he was suddenly roused by a terrible noise : "The staircase is burning ! The staircase is in flames !" cried the young rogues. In a second Gray was out of bed, he threw open the window, fastened the ladder, and got to the ground as quickly as he could. But suddenly, he felt himself in an ice-cold bath, for the rogues had placed a tub of water below to receive him. The joke cured Gray of his fear of fire, but he could never forgive it.

LIV.

An English wine-merchant, who was purveyor to George III., was such a favorite with the king that he was sometimes invited to take part in the Royal Hunt. One day, returning from the chase, the king entered into conversation with him, and rode by his side for some distance. Lord Walsingham, who was in the king's suite, noticed that the wine-merchant was lacking in respect towards his sovereign, and was remarking to the man, in a whisper, that he had not taken off his hat before the king, when the king overheard him. "What's that, what's that, Walsingham?" inquired the good-humored monarch. Before the nobleman had time to answer, the merchant said eagerly: "I find that I have been guilty of disrespect to your majesty, in not taking off my hat. But your majesty will please to observe that whenever I hunt, my hat is fastened to my wig, and my wig to my head, and I am on the back of a spirited horse; so that if I take anything off, I must go off myself." It is needless to say that this artless apology was accepted.

LV.

Bismarck was once in the park at St. Petersburg, and met the emperor there. They walked a certain distance together, when they came to a lawn in the middle of which stood a sentry. Bismarck took the liberty of asking what he was there for. The emperor did not know, and asked his aide-de-camp, but the latter did not know either. "Then ask the sentry himself," said the emperor. The sentry only answered: "That's the command." This information, however, was not of much use, and the aide-de-camp had to apply to the officer of the guards, and then to some one of a higher rank. But the reply was always the same: "That's the command." They looked it up in the records, but found nothing about the matter—a sentry *always* stood there. Finally, an old lackey is found, who remembers that his father, also an old lackey, once told him that the Empress Catherine once found an early snowdrop at that spot, and gave orders that it should not be plucked. They knew no better way of taking care of it than by placing a sentry there, and there a sentry had always remained.

LVI.

Benjamin Franklin, the well-known American statesman and philosopher, relates the following story of his boyhood. One cold winter morning he was accosted by a man with an axe on his shoulder. "My pretty boy," said he with a smile, "has your father a grindstone?"—"Yes, sir," said Franklin.—"You are a fine little fellow," said he; "will you let me sharpen my axe on it." Pleased with being called a fine little fellow, Franklin answered: "O yes, it is down in the shed." Patting the little boy on the head, the man added: "And will you get a little water for me to wet the grindstone?" Little[1]

---

[1] Translate, "the little."

Benjamin, unable to resist the flattering manners of the stranger, at once complied, and soon returned with a pailful of water. "How old are you, and what's your name?" continued the man, without waiting for a reply. "I am sure you are one of the finest lads that I have ever seen. Will you just turn the grindstone for me for a few minutes?" Delighted with the compliments paid him, young Benjamin went to work, but he was soon sorry for being so simple. The axe was a dull one, and he had to toil till his arms were aching.

LVII.

La Fontaine used to eat a baked apple every evening. Once when he was called out of the room he laid the apple on the mantelpiece. During his absence a visitor came into the room, saw the apple and ate it. When La Fontaine came back, and did not find the apple, he guessed what had become of it, and exclaimed with feigned astonishment: "Where is the apple gone that I left here?"—"I don't know," said the other.—"I am glad to hear that, for I had put arsenic in it to poison rats."—"Good heavens! I am poisoned," exclaimed the visitor, extremely terrified; "send at once for the doctor!"—"Good friend," said La Fontaine, "compose yourself; I remember now that I forgot this time to put poison in. I am sorry, however, that a lie was necessary to discover the truth."

LVIII.

When the Emperor Joseph II. was in Paris in the reign of Louis XVI., he was in the habit of walking about the city incognito. One morning he went into an elegant coffee-house, and asked for a cup of chocolate. He was plainly dressed, and the waiters insolently refused to give it, saying it was too early. Without making any reply, he walked out, and went into a little coffee-house. He asked for a cup of chocolate, and the landlord politely answered that it would be ready in a moment. While he waited for it, as there were no customers in the coffee-house, he walked up and down, and was conversing on different subjects, when the landlord's daughter, a very pretty girl, entered the room. The Emperor wished her a good day, according to the French mode; and observed to her father that it was time she was married. "Ah!" replied the old man, "if I had only[1] a thousand crowns, I could marry her to a man who is very fond of her—but, sir—the chocolate is ready." The Emperor called for pen, ink and paper: the girl ran to fetch them; and he gave her an order on his banker for six thousand livres.

LIX.

When the "Utopia" of Sir Thomas More was first published, it occasioned an amusing mistake. This political romance represents a perfect but visionary

---

[1] Translate by *seulement*.

republic in an island supposed to have been newly discovered in America. "As this was the age of discovery[1]"; says Granger, "the learned Budæus and others took it for a genuine history, and considered it[2] as highly expedient that missionaries should be sent thither, in order to convert so wise a nation to Christianity."

LX.

Domenichino, the Italian painter, was accustomed to act the parts of the personages he wished to represent on his canvas,[3] and to speak aloud the words which he conceived to be used by these figures. When he was painting the martyrdom of St. Andrew, Carracci one day caught him in a violent passion, speaking in a furious and menacing tone. He was at that moment employed in painting a soldier who was threatening the saint. As soon as this fit of abstraction had passed, Carraci ran and embraced him, acknowledging that Domenichino had this time been his master, and had taught him how to catch the true expression of his faces.

LXI.

A somewhat similar story is told of Crébillon, the celebrated French tragic poet, who was fond of shutting himself in, that he might weave his romantic

---

[1] Use the plural.
[2] Omit.
[3] Use the plural.

plots in peace. One day, when he was in a deep reverie, a friend entered abruptly. "Don't disturb me," cried the poet, "I am enjoying a moment of happiness: I am going to hang a villain of a[1] minister, and banish another who is an idiot."

LXII.

Longfellow, the American poet, was noted for his kindness to children. Among those who came oftenest to see him there was a little boy of whom he was very fond. One day when this child was in the library, he examined intently the rows of books and at last asked: "Have you got 'Jack the Giant-Killer'?"

Longfellow had to confess that he had[2] not. The little boy looked at the poet with an expression of great regret, and presently slipped down from his knee and went away.

The next morning Longfellow saw him coming towards the house with something tightly clasped in his little hands. He had brought a ten-cent piece with which the poet was to buy a "Jack the Giant-Killer" of his own.

LXIII.

A German professor went for a ride one day. When he was outside the town, he took a book from

---

[1] Omit.
[2] Supply the object.

his pocket and began to read. He soon became completely absorbed in his reading, and did not notice that his horse shied and threw him into the ditch. He was still sitting where he had fallen when an acquaintance happened to pass that way, and asked him what he was doing there. The good professor, annoyed at the interruption, looked up and said crabbedly: "Dear me, can't you see that I am taking a ride?"

LXIV.

While in Paris, Garrick and his friend Preville hired a coach to go Versailles. They got in and ordered the coachman to drive on. "Not yet," said he, "I want two more passengers."—"All right," said Garrick, "we shall wait." But a few minutes after, he slipped out, went round the coach, passed himself off to the coachman for a stranger and got in again. He got out a second time, and in again with the same success. He tried it a third time, but the coachman said gruffly: "Away with you! Don't you see I am full?" And he would have driven off without him, had Preville not called out that, as the stranger was very small, they would contrive to make room for him.

LXV.

The *Liverpool Post* contains a good story of Lord Houghton and Lord Tennyson. Lord Houghton was invited to dine at seven, an[1] hour which was particularly disagreeable to him. He came, however, and was placed on his host's left hand, with Lord Tennyson on the right. Presently the Poet Laureate, much absorbed as usual in his own affairs, complained that he could not anywhere get a copy of his earliest poems. Hearing this, Lord Houghton, who had remained very silent, woke up and gruffly remarked: "Oh, I can give you a copy. I've made a collection of all the rubbish you ever wrote, and when you're[2] dead I'll publish it to spite you." However, Lord Houghton died first.

LXVI.

Henry Ward Beecher tells us that he never saw anybody occupied in doing anything, without watching to see how it was done, since he might some day be obliged to do it himself. This habit of observation once stood him in good stead.

"I was going," he says, "across a prairie when my horse began to limp. Luckily I came across a blacksmith's shop, but the smith was not at home. I asked his wife if she would allow me to start a fire and make a shoe. She gave me permission to do it. So I started the fire and heated the shoe red-hot, and shaped it to my horse's foot, and pared the hoofs and bent the points of the nails, as I had seen the blacksmith do, so that, in driving them into the hoof they

---

[1] Omit.
[2] Use the future.

should not get into the quick, and I shod the horse. At the next village I went to a smith and told him to put the shoe on properly. He looked at the horse's foot and paid me the greatest compliment I ever received in my life. He told me if I had put on that shoe I had better become a blacksmith altogether. Now I should never have known how to do that if I had not carefully observed others."

LXVII.

A gentleman who had borne many troubles without complaining, said to a friend who asked him to reveal the secret of being always so patient and happy: "Very willingly, my friend. It consists simply in making a right use of my eyes, whatever may be my condition. I first look up to heaven, and remember that my principal business is to get there. Then I look down upon the earth, and call to mind how small a space I shall occupy in it when my life is[1] done. And lastly, I look at the world around me and observe how many there are who, in all respects, are more unhappy than I. In this way I learn where true happiness is to be found, where all my cares must end, and how little cause I have to complain."

LXVIII.

The Duke of Edinburgh, Queen Victoria's second son, has become Duke of Saxe-Coburg-Gotha, and the newspapers are telling many stories about him. Here

---

[1] Use the future.

is one of them. When the duke was commanding the *Galatea* he went one day to visit an admiral. As he was not wearing his uniform, the admiral, on receiving him, said: "I should have been glad to receive your Royal Highness at any other time, but, unfortunately, at this moment, I am expecting a visit from the captain of the *Galatea*." The duke returned to his ship and put on his uniform.

In another story it is related that when he was travelling in Canada he had a guide who had served his brother in eighteen hundred and sixty. The guide one day remarked: "The Prince of Wales gave me a fine gold watch, sir."—"Indeed," said Prince Alfred, "that is something he has never done for me."

LXIX.

In the time of Joe Miller, there was an old deaf actor of the name of Cross, who was very vain and who took every pains to conceal his infirmity. Joe, walking along Fleet Street with a friend, saw Cross on[1] the opposite side, and told his companion that he should see some fine sport. So, beckoning to Cross, he opened his mouth wide and acted as if he were bawling very loud to some one at a distance. Cross thought that Miller had hallooed to him, and taking that as too public an indication of his deafness, rushed across the street out of breath and cried to Joe: "Why the deuce are you making such a noise? Do you think people can't hear?"

---

[1] Use *de*.

LXX.

The proud Duke of Somerset employed Seymour the painter to make some portraits of his race-horses. One day at dinner the Duke drank to him with a sneer, saying: "Cousin Seymour, your health!" The painter replied: "I really do believe that I have the honor to be of your Grace's family." The duke, offended, rose from table, and sent his steward to pay the painter and dismiss him. Another artist was sent for, who, finding himself unable to finish Seymour's work, honestly told the Duke so. On this the haughty peer condescended once more to summon his cousin. But Seymour answered in these words: "My Lord, I shall now prove that I am of your Grace's family, for I will not come."

LXXI.

There is a well-known story of Alain Chartier, the French poet, and Margaret of Scotland, the wife of the Dauphin, who afterwards was Louis XI.

Alain was extremely plain-looking, but his poetry had won the affection of the princess. One day, passing through a hall in the palace, where he was lying asleep on a bench, she approached and kissed him. When her attendants expressed their amazement that she should have kissed the lips of a man so dreadfully ugly, she turned and said with a smile: "It was not the man that I kissed, but those precious lips from which have issued so many witticisms and virtuous sentences."

LXXII.

The other day, a certain foreign countess was questioning her son's tutor regarding the boy's progress. "How does the Viscount get on?" said she.—"Wonderfully well, my lady; we are hard at work at the sciences. The Viscount is particularly well up in chemistry."—"Indeed! Ah! then, Henri, my child, do tell me what is[1] dynamite."—"Pardon me, madame," interrupted the tutor, "but nowadays dynamite does not belong to chemistry; it is considered a part and parcel of political economy."

LXXIII.

John Abernethy, the celebrated surgeon, was a man of very few words, and was pleased when he met a patient as laconic as himself. One day a lady entered his consulting room, and, without saying "Good morning," showed him the first finger of her left hand. The following conversation took place: "Cut?"—"Bite."—"Dog?"—"Parrot."—"Bread poultice." And so ended the first conversation.

On the second visit, the lady, without uttering a word, lifted up her finger, which[2] was the signal for the following dialogue: "Better?"—"Worse."—"Linseed poultice."

On the third visit, it was simply: "Better?"—"Well." But when the lady was about to pay the

---

[1] *Ce que c'est que.* See page 2, note 1.
[2] *Ce qui.*

doctor, he burst out: "Fees! Not for the world. You are a most sensible woman. You don't speak. Adieu."

LXXIV.

Some merchants went to an Eastern sovereign and offered to sell him several very fine horses. The king admired the handsome animals and bought them. Then he gave the merchants a sum of money to purchase more horses for him. One day not long after, the king jokingly ordered his vizier to make out a list of all the fools in his dominions. When the list was completed, the king found his own name at the head of it. He asked the vizier the reason of this, and the man replied: "Because you entrusted a quantity of money to men whom you don't know and who will never come back."—"Ah! but what[1] if they do come back?"—"Oh! then I shall strike out your name and put in theirs."

LXXV.

A French bishop was once travelling in a stage-coach, in company with a commercial traveller. The latter, wishing to divert himself at the expense of the reverend gentleman, asked him this question: "What is the difference between an ass and a bishop?" The bishop was so surprised that he looked for a moment at the impertinent fellow without saying a word. Then he said, quietly and

---

[1] Omit.

politely: "I really do not know, sir."—"It is," replies his companion, "that an ass wears his cross on his back, while the bishop wears his on his breast."—"And you sir," says the good bishop in his turn, "do you know what the difference is between an ass and a commercial traveller?"—"No."—"Well, no more do I."

LXXVI.

It is related that when the Duke of Orleans was Regent, a certain man of talent was very anxious to present a petition to him. He seized a moment when the Duke was at leisure and almost alone, and presented his petition drawn up in the usual form. When the Regent had read it, the petitioner said: "If your Highness would read it again, here it is in verse."—"Willingly," said the Duke, "give it me." The reading of the verses being ended, the man asked permission to sing it. He was allowed to do so. No sooner had he finished singing than he said: "If your Highness wishes, I will dance it."—"Oh! dance it," answered the Regent, "and, for the novelty of the feat, I will grant you what you ask."

LXXVII.

Paul saddled his horse to go and carry his rent to the landlord of the farm he occupied. When he was about to mount, he saw that there was a nail wanting in one of the shoes. "It is not worth while to replace it," said he to himself, "for want of a nail my horse won't give out on the way."

A league from home, Paul saw that the horse had lost the shoe in which the nail was wanting. "I could easily get another shoe put on at the neighboring smithy," said he, "but I should lose too much time; my horse will reach town well enough with three shoes."

Soon after, the horse stepped on a thorn and wounded himself. "I might get my beast attended to," said Paul to himself once more, "but it isn't more than a quarter of a league from here to the town. He will finish the journey well enough as he is."

A few minutes after, the horse in limping made a false step and fell. Paul was thrown to the ground with such violence that he dislocated his shoulder. He was carried to a village near by, where man and horse had to be nursed for ten days. Paul was much distressed at thus losing his time and his money. Then he said to himself: "There are no such things as trifling oversights. If I had put a nail in, my horse would not have lost his shoe; if I had had a a shoe put on, he would not have hurt himself; if I had had his wound dressed in time, I should not have put my shoulder out of joint. This lesson will be useful to me for the future."

LXXVIII.

A nightingale had all day enlivened the village with his song, and at night-fall was singing still. However, he was getting hungry and looked around him for something to eat. At some distance he saw a bluish light on the ground, like a little star fallen from the sky. The nightingale had seen this little light before, and knew that it came from a glowworm. So he flew down from his branch in the top of a hawthorn, intending to devour the worm at a single mouthful. But the worm, guessing his intention, addressed him as follows: "If you admired my light as much as I admire your song, you would have a horror of doing me harm, as I have[1] of spoiling your melody. For it was the same divine power that created us both, and taught you to sing and me to shine, so that you by your music and I with my spark should lighten and cheer the night."

The songster was completely won over, warbled out his approbation, and, leaving the glowworm to shine in peace, he took flight to find his supper somewhere else.

LXXIX.

Turenne, the great French general, was born in 1611 and was killed in 1675. He was a man of heroic character, and was as upright, generous and humane as he was brave. Seeing a wounded soldier, exhausted by hunger and fatigue, lying where he had fallen at the foot of a tree and in danger of being killed by the enemy, this great general dismounted, lifted him on to his horse, and followed on foot, at the risk of being captured by the horsemen who were pursuing him.

[1] Omit.

At another time, the inhabitants of a German town having come to offer him a large sum not to quarter his troops upon them, he replied to them: "Keep your money; your town is not on the route I am to follow."

Having had the weakness to let slip a state secret which the king, Louis XIV., had entrusted only to him and the minister Louvois, he learned that the latter was suspected. Turenne went at once and confessed his fault before the king with great repentance.

When he had won a battle (and he won many) he used to say: "We have gained a victory," associating all his companions in arms with successes which were due but to him. And when he suffered a defeat, which rarely happened to him, he wrote: "I have been beaten." France saw in him her greatest warrior and her best defender. He was known and loved by the whole nation.

LXXX.

A father told this story to his little son, who had been so much afraid of a goat that he had cried.

I was once quite as silly as you; and I was older. I was eight years old. We lived in the country at the sea-side. In front of the house there was a lawn. I had just been ill, and they had put me in the drawing-room on the ground floor. I was stretched on a sofa, waiting for the return of my mother who had gone to bathe, and I was reading the tale of "Little

Red Riding-Hood." The heat was stifling. The thunder was rumbling in the distance, and the sea with great noise was rolling the shingle on the beach. The window was open; and the wind which precedes a storm was shaking the lowered blind. Suddenly the blind rose, and I saw a horrible black face, with two big eyes that were looking at me, and an enormous mouth with long teeth opened as if to swallow me. It was certainly the wolf, and I was little Red Riding-Hood. I wanted to cry out, to call; but I had no voice. The blind had fallen back again, but I knew the horrible face was there behind it.[1] Fortunately the monster took the notion to speak: "Hee haw! hee haw!" It had come for the piece of sugar I used to give it after my ride. It was only the old she-ass, who was looking kindly at me when I raised the blind again. So I got off with a good scare.

LXXXI.

Once upon a time there was a little girl who was much given to idleness. She had a fairy godmother (there were still some in those times), and she asked her godmother for one or two little servants, as clever and as industrious as she was the opposite.

"I shall give you neither one nor two," said the godmother, "but ten, whom you will only have to command, and who will obey you in a moment. Once they are trained to serve you, they will dress

---

[1] Omit.

you, wash you, do up your hair, sew, embroider for you, only I can't let you have them longer than a week."

The little girl could not contain herself for joy. The ten little fairies obeyed her in everything. At the end of the week the godmother came back, and said: "Well, are you satisfied?"—"Yes," said the child, but I can no longer do without my dear little fairies. What will become of me without them?"—"I see but one way of leaving them with you," said the godmother, "that is, to fasten one to each of your fingers." This was done and the little lazy girl became in a short time the most skilful workwoman.

LXXXII.

Some time since, the following advertisement appeared in a Paris newspaper: "Infallible means of making fifty francs a week with an outlay of ten francs. Send three francs in postage-stamps to ——; and the receipt will be sent by return of post."

A young man, in search of a standing in society, wrote to the address indicated, and took care to enclose in his letter the three francs required. The reply reached him next day. Here it is: "Buy a sack of potatoes, cut them up, fry them and sell them again in portions. You will realise by this operation in one week a clear profit of fifty francs."

LXXXIII.

On the railway line from Berlin to Breslau, a gentleman entered a second-class compartment in which there were a number of other passengers. He at once noticed an unpleasant odor, and soon discovered a piece of old Limburg cheese, wrapped in paper and lying on the luggage-rack. Each of the travellers, supposing that the cheese belonged to one of the others, sat in ill-natured silence, regretting that he was not somewhere else. Not a word was spoken during the long journey, and at last they reached Breslau. The train had scarcely stopped when the carriage door was opened from the outside by a big good-natured Saxon, who said: "Beg pardon, gentlemen, the cheese is mine. I put it here because it smelt a trifle too strong in my compartment." So saying, the Saxon walked away with the parcel under his arm, followed by the loud laughter of the passengers.

LXXXIV.

A villager was one day looking very thoughtfully at a pumpkin of extraordinary size. "Truly," said he at last, "the Author of nature did not know what he was doing when he attached this fruit to so slender a stem. If I had been in his place, I should have set it on one of those oaks I see yonder in the forest. Why, for instance, does not an acorn, which is not so large as my finger, grow on that small plant? The more I look at those two fruits, the more it seems to me that God has made a mistake."

After speaking in this way, the villager went and lay down under an oak and fell asleep. The wind was blowing. An acorn fell on his nose and awoke him. He suddenly brings his hand to his face, seizes the acorn, looks at it with astonishment and notices a faint mark of blood. "What is this?" he exclaims, "Oh! my nose is bleeding! But what a lucky thing it was only an acorn! I should have had a pretty nose if a pumpkin had fallen on it. I see after all that Providence is not so stupid as I thought a moment ago."

LXXXV.

The following story is told by a celebrated French painter, still living. A certain painting by Jean François Millet had attracted attention enough to render it worthy of being engraved. The engraver, on receiving it, took it from its frame, wrapped it in an old newspaper, and left it in the porter's lodge in the house where he lived. When he came back to go up to his rooms, he completely forgot the picture, and it was only after nearly a fortnight that he remembered having received it. He searched high and low through his rooms, but found no trace of it. He was naturally a little uneasy, knowing that, however insignificant the picture might be as a work of art, the poor painter no doubt prized it highly. While the engraver was in this distress, the porter told him there was a troublesome canvas knocking about his lodge, which he did not like to throw away, and so Millet's picture came to light again. Its subsequent history is known to everybody, for it was the famous painting of the Angelus.

LXXXVI.

A certain judge of Avignon, famous for his love of good cheer, said one day to a friend: "We have just been dining off a splendid turkey. It was excellent; stuffed with truffles to the very throat, tender and delicate. We left nothing but the bones."—"And how many were there of you?" asked the friend. "Two," replied the judge. — "Two?" echoed the other in amazement. — "Yes, two," repeated the judge, "the turkey and myself."

LXXXVII.

One day a plainly dressed elderly lady, caught in a shower, took refuge in a little cottage, belonging to a poor peasant woman. "Good day, my good woman," said she to her, "I have been caught in the country by the rain. Would you do me the favor to lend me an umbrella to get home?" The country-woman looked askance at her visitor, and, after some hesitation, said to her: "I have two umbrellas; one a silk one,[1] quite new and very pretty, but that one you shall not have.[2] I am going to keep it for myself; I should not be very sure of seeing it again. Here, take the other." And she gave the lady an old umbrella, all full of holes, with the whalebones coming out here and there through the cloth. "Thank you, ma'am. That is better than nothing,"

---

[1] Translate, "the one in silk."
[2] Supply, "it."

said the stranger. "That will protect me a little at all events."

The next morning the countrywoman received a visit from a handsome footman all covered with lace. He brought back the umbrella with the thanks of the Queen. "Good gracious!" cried the woman, "was that the Queen, then, who came yesterday evening and borrowed an umbrella of me?"—"It was the Queen herself."—"Why didn't she tell me so at first?"— "Why so?"—"Because... because... if I had known, I should have lent her my new umbrella, and given[1] her anything else she had[2] asked me for."

LXXXVIII.

Marshal Lefebvre one day received a visit from an old comrade in arms. The visitor admired, with some feeling of envy, the marshal's handsome residence, his liveried servants, in fine, all the style and dignity of the Empire. "Upon my word," said he to his old comrade, "you must admit that you are very lucky and that Heaven has treated you well."— "Do you want to have all that?" said the marshal. —"Yes, certainly I do," said his guest.—"Very good, the thing is very simple. You will go down into the court. I shall place at each window two soldiers who will fire at you. If you escape the bullets, I will give you all you envy me. That's the way I got it."

---

[1] Repeat the subject and the auxiliary.
[2] Use the conditional.

LXXXIX.

A countryman was going one day to the town, followed by his son, little[1] Thomas. "Look!" said he to his son on the way, "there is a piece of a horse-shoe lying on the ground; pick it up and put it in your pocket."—"Pshaw!" said little[1] Tom, "it isn't worth while to stoop and pick it up." His father made no reply, took the piece of iron and put it in his pocket. In the next village he sold it to the blacksmith, and bought cherries with the money.

They continued on their way. It was very warm. Tom was dying with thirst and had the greatest difficulty in[2] following his father. The latter dropped a cherry, as if by accident. Tom picked it up with great avidity and put it quickly into his mouth. A few steps farther, a second cherry fell on the ground, which Tom swallowed with the same eagerness. This was repeated until he had picked up all the cherries.

When he had eaten the last one, his father turned to him laughing and said: "You see now that if you had been willing to stoop once for the horse-shoe, you would not have been obliged to do it a score of times for the cherries."

XC.

An ass, accompanied by a dog, was carrying bread to market, and their master was following. As they

---

[1] See note, page 44.
[2] Use à followed by the infinitive.

were passing through a meadow, the latter lay down and fell asleep, and the ass began to graze. "Friend," said the dog, "I have not dined to-day; and grass, you know, is not my food. Bend down a little; I should like to take a roll from[1] your basket." As the ass makes no reply, the dog repeats his request. But he speaks in vain; his companion turns a deaf ear to him. At length the ass stops cropping the grass, and says to the dog: "I advise you to wait. Our master will not be long before he wakes, and then he will give you your dinner."

During this conversation, a hungry wolf came out of a neighbouring wood. "My dear friend, defend me," cries the ass in terror.—"Comrade," replies the dog in his turn, "I advise you to wait till our master is awake, he won't be long." Thereupon the dog scampers off, and the wolf strangles the ass.

XCI.

A wasp met a bee and said to her: "Pray, can you tell me why men are so ill-natured to me, while they are so fond of you? We are very much alike, although I have gold on my body that makes me handsomer than you. We are both winged insects, we both love honey, and we both sting people when we are angry. Yet men always hate me and try to kill me, though I am much more familiar with them than

---

[1] Use *dans*. The verb *prendre* being used here in its primitive, etymological sense of "seize," "grasp," it takes the preposition which marks *rest in* rather than *motion from*. Cf. *Il a pris l'argent dans sa poche. Il a pris son chapeau sur la table,* etc.

you are, and pay them visits in their houses. You, on the other hand, are very shy and hardly ever come near them; yet they build you curious houses, thatched with straw, and take care of you, and feed you in the winter very often. I wonder what is the reason."

Then the bee replied: "Because you never do them any good; but, on the contrary, are very troublesome and mischievous. It is no wonder they don't like to see you. But they know that I am busy all day long, making them honey. You had better pay them fewer visits, and try to be useful."

XCII.

A young mouse lived in a cupboard where sweetmeats were kept. She dined every day upon biscuit, marmalade or fine sugar. Never had any little mouse[1] lived so well. She would have been quite happy, if it had not been for the cat, who sometimes frightened her, and made her run trembling to her hole behind the wainscot.

One day she came running to her mother in great joy. "Mother," said she, "the good people of this family have built me a house to live in. It is in the cupboard. I am sure it is for me, for it is just big enough. The floor is of wood and the walls are of wire. I don't doubt that they have made it on purpose to hide me from that terrible cat, which runs

---

[1] Translate, "Never little mouse had, etc."

after me so often. There is an entrance just big enough to let me in, but puss can't follow me. Then they have been so good as to put in some toasted cheese, which smells so delicious that I should have liked to run in directly and take possession of my new house; but I thought I would tell you first, that we might both go in together, for it will hold us both."

"My dear child," said the old mouse, "it is most fortunate that you did not go in; for that house is a trap, and you would never have come out again. Beware of things which seem to be made for our comfort."

XCIII.

A merchant who died some time ago, leaving a large sum of money, was so great a miser that for many years he ate nothing for his breakfast and his dinner except a dry crust of bread. And, what is more, he obliged his son, a young boy about twelve years old, to live upon the same food.

However, he was one day tempted by what a friend said to him of the nice taste of cheese, and he bought[1] a small piece. But before he got home, he began to reproach himself for spending[2] so much money, and instead of eating the cheese, he put it into a bottle, and thought it was more than enough

---

[1] Add, "of it."
[2] Translate, "having spent."

to rub his bread against the bottle. His poor son was, of course, forced to do the same.

One day, on coming home later than usual, he found the boy eating[1] his crust and[2] rubbing it against the door. "What are you doing, you[3] fool?" he cried.—"It is dinner-time, father," said the boy, "but you have the key, and I could not open the door. So I was rubbing my bread against it, because I could not get to the bottle."—"Can't you go without cheese one day, you[3] greedy boy? You will never be rich." And as he said this, he kicked the poor fellow for not being able to eat his bread without cheese.

---
[1] Translate, "who was eating."
[2] "And" may be replaced by *en* followed by the present participle.
[3] Omit.

PART III.—HISTORICAL AND BIOGRAPHICAL SKETCHES.

I.

Clovis is frequently regarded as the first king of France. Although this may not be quite exact, it was he who first, after the fall of the Roman Empire, tried to unite into one kingdom all the parts into which France was at that time divided. By the death of his father in 481 A.D., he became king of the Salian Franks, who held the eastern part of France. His first achievement was the defeat of the Gallo-Romans, who inhabited the territory around Paris. In a battle near Soissons he defeated their king, Syagrius, and established himself in that town. In 493 he married Clotilda, daughter of a prince of Burgundy. This princess was a Christian and she desired earnestly that Clovis might be converted to Christianity. He did not yield at first, but, one day, while struggling with his enemies, the Alemanni, at the battle of Tolbiac, he cried out in his distress that if God would grant him the victory, he would become a Christian. Victory was granted, and, on the following Christmas day, Clovis and many of his soldiers were baptised by St. Remi, bishop of Rheims. The pope conferred on him the title of "The Most Christian King," and he showed great zeal in the defence of the faith. In 507 he undertook an expedition against Alaric II., king of the Visigoths, who were heretics, and he defeated and slew that monarch at a battle near Poitiers. Clovis then made Paris his capital, and died there in 511.

II.

Charlemagne is one of the most famous names in history. He was the grandson of the famous Charles Martel (Charles the Hammer), who saved Europe on the battle-field of Tours in 732. Charlemagne well deserves the name *great* (magnus) which he bears. He was great in war. He conquered the Saxons on the east of his kingdom, and the Lombards on the south. He crossed the Pyrenees also and inflicted chastisement on the Moors. He extended his empire from the Ebro to the Elbe. He was great also in peace. He encouraged education, agriculture, arts, manufactures and commerce, and gave to his subjects good laws and institutions. In the year 800 he went to Rome to aid the Pope in quelling a rebellion in that city, and, while worshipping on Christmas day in St. Peter's church, was crowned by the Pope as Carolus Augustus, Emperor of the Romans. He returned to his capital, Aix-la-Chapelle, a town still existing in Western Prussia, and exercised still greater authority and enjoyed still greater renown on account of his new title. At length, on the 28th of January 814, he died in his capital and was buried in the chapel which he had built. He left behind various Latin writings: laws, letters and even poems. But above all, his great renown filled French literature during many generations. His deeds and those of his family and friends are the subject of many of the celebrated epic poems of the Middle Ages, often called the *chansons de geste*, the greatest of which is the *Chanson de Roland*.

III.

Louis IX., or Saint Louis as he is generally called, was a king whose memory is highly venerated by the French people. He was born in 1215 and succeeded his father, Louis VIII., in 1226; his mother, Blanche of Castile, being regent during his youth. He engaged in war with Henry III. of England, and gained some advantage over the latter. During a dangerous illness he made a vow, that, if he recovered, he would organize a crusade and accompany it in person. Accordingly he set sail in 1248 for Egypt, intending to go on to Palestine later. He took Damietta but was afterwards taken prisoner by the Mohammedans. He returned to France and remained there till 1270, when he embarked on a new crusade. But when the expedition was at Tunis on its way to Palestine, a pestilence broke out and the king died of it. Louis is renowned for his justice, kindness and piety. Like a true father of his people, he is said to have administered justice sitting under an oak tree in the forest of Vincennes. But he did more. He established courts in all parts of his kingdom, and made a code of laws known as the *Établisse-ments de Saint Louis*. One of the most famous institutions founded in his reign was the Sorbonne, at first a sort of boarding-house for poor students, afterwards one of the great universities of the world. He built also the beautiful little church called the Sainte-Chapelle, in which he placed the holy relics which he brought back from the East. The story of his life and deeds has been preserved in the *Vie de Saint Louis*, written by his friend and companion Jean de Joinville.

IV.

Henry IV., surnamed "the Good," and "the Great," has been called the most French of all the French kings. The large number of anecdotes which exist regarding his kindliness and unaffected manners, shows us that he holds a large place in the affections of the French people. Henry was bred a Protestant, and, in the beginning of his career, was the leader of the Huguenot party. Brave and talented, he led his party with success for a time, and inflicted defeats on his enemies. Born in 1553, he became king in 1589, on the death of Henry III., and continued his victorious career against the Catholic party. But he was no less prudent than brave, and finding that he would never be accepted heartily by the majority of the nation, so long as he remained a Protestant, he abjured Protestantism, and publicly proclaimed himself a Catholic in the Church of St. Denis, in 1593.

This act secured for him the affection of the Catholics and did not destroy the allegiance of the Protestants, to whom he granted liberty of faith by the proclamation of the celebrated Edict of Nantes in 1598. Henry then busied himself with the affairs of his kingdom. He corrected abuses of all kinds in the government of the people. He made good roads and canals in order to facilitate trade. He paid attention to the condition of the poor, and said he would not be satisfied, as long as every man in his kingdom could not have a good chicken in his pot on Sunday. And he did not confine his energies to the politics of his own country. He was a mediator of treaties of peace between other nations, and it is said he was meditating the establishment of a Christian republic in Europe. But, in the midst of all his plans for the good of humanity, his life was cut short by the assassin Ravaillac, who stabbed him in his coach, on the 14th of May 1610.

v.

The reign of Louis XIV. is the longest and the most glorious in French history. It extends from 1643 to 1715. Louis was but five years old when he began to reign, and during his minority his mother, Anne of Austria, was regent. In 1660, when Louis was twenty-two, he married the Infanta of Spain and took into his own hands the reins of government. By the help of his great generals, such as Condé, Turenne and Luxembourg, he extended the territory of France towards the east. No nation of Europe was able to cope with him in war, in the first part of his reign; but in the later years of his life the English under Marlborough defeated the French armies in a number of battles in the Low Countries. The government of Louis was quite despotic. His famous saying, "L'état c'est moi," gives us an exact idea of the principles upon which his government was based. One of the worst blots upon the fame of Louis was caused by the revocation of the Edict of Nantes in 1685. From that time on, the Protestants suffered great persecution. The greatest glory of the reign is that which is due to the wonderful group of writers who adorned it. No period of French history has produced so many great men. The comedies of Molière, the tragedies of Racine and Corneille, the satires of Boileau, the fables of La Fontaine, and the sermons of Bossuet, have never been surpassed by the works of any writers who have lived since.

VI.

Napoleon Bonaparte, one of the greatest military geniuses the world has ever seen, was born in Corsica in 1769. He was educated in the military schools of Brienne and Paris, and was proficient in mathematics, but was weak in Latin and the accomplishments. At the siege of Toulon he distinguished himself, and in 1796 was appointed general of the Army of Italy. With his army he proceeded into that country, and defeated Italians and Austrians in several important battles, such as Lodi and Arcola. After this followed his celebrated expedition to Egypt, in which he won some victories, but whose general result was unimportant. On the 18th of Brumaire (November 9th) 1799, he expelled the members of the Legislature from the chamber in which it was sitting, and became First Consul shortly after. From this time on, he was absolute ruler of France, although he was not crowned Emperor till 1804. From 1800 till about 1812, his career was a long series of brilliant victories. During that period he humbled the pride of Russia, Prussia, and Austria in such battles as Marengo, Austerlitz, Jena, Eylau and Wagram. But in 1812, he led his ill-fated expedition into Russia. The Russians set fire to Moscow, and Napoleon was forced to retreat to France, to escape the rigors of the Russian winter. Only a few thousands of the French soldiers returned home. At the same time, the Spaniards, aided by the English under Wellington, harassed the French armies in the Peninsula. The result of these reverses was that Napoleon abdicated and retired to the Island of Elba in 1814. In a few months, however, he returned to France, and reorganized his army. Having marched into Belgium, he met the English and Prussian armies at Waterloo, and was defeated on the 18th of June 1815. He was then sent as a prisoner of war to St. Helena, a lonely rock in the Atlantic Ocean, at some distance from the west coast of Africa, where he died on the 5th of May 1821. His remains were brought back to France in 1840 and placed in a magnificent tomb in the Hôtel des Invalides, in Paris.

VII.

Few personages of history have served so frequently as subjects for writers and artists, as Joan of Arc, and no name awakens so strongly the patriotic sentiments of Frenchmen of our day. She was born in 1412, in the little village of Domremy, in Lorraine. Her parents were poor, and the only instruction she received was in the simple occupations of her peasant life. But as she kept her sheep, she would think of the stories of the Bible and of the Lives of the Saints, and she herself had visions from Heaven. She brooded, too, over the sorrows of poor France, at that time under the domination of the English, and she conceived the idea of freeing her native land from the stranger. After having conquered the scruples of her countrymen, she put herself at the head of an army of Frenchmen and marched to the relief of Orleans, which was being besieged by the English. After fifteen days of fighting, the English were compelled to raise the siege and to retreat, ascribing their defeat to witchcraft. The French nation acquired new courage from the contemplation of her heroism, and the cowardly Dauphin allowed himself to be crowned Charles VII., in the cathedral of Rheims under the inspiration of her courage. But at the siege of Compiègne she was abandoned by her own troops and was taken prisoner. She was led to Rouen, where she was tried as a sorceress and condemned to death by the English. On the 30th of May 1431, she was burned at the stake, a real martyr, in the midst of the insults of her enemies.

VIII.

Victor Hugo, the greatest French poet of the nineteenth century, was born in 1802 in Besançon, a town in the east of France. He commenced to write poetry when he was very young, winning honors at a poetical competition held at Toulouse, called the *Jeux-Floraux*, when he was only seventeen years of age. When he was twenty, he published his first volume of poetry, and the world recognized that a remarkable genius had appeared. Before he was thirty years of age he had produced several volumes of lyric poetry, several plays, and several romances. The most important of these plays was the tragedy *Hernani*, which was produced on the 25th of February 1830, at the Théatre Français. In writing this play, Hugo had violated the rules of the drama which had been followed by all the great writers of tragedy for two hundred years; and so its production made a great commotion amongst the critics. After 1830, Hugo continued to write, producing amongst other things his celebrated romance *Notre Dame de Paris*, in 1831, and he became more and more renowned. In 1841, he became a member of the French Academy, the greatest honor conferred by

Frenchmen on a writer. He began also to take part in politics, and during the Second Republic, which lasted from 1848 till 1851, he was one of the most important public men of the nation. The *Coup d'État* of December 1851, drove him from France, and he became an exile, living in Belgium, Jersey and Guernsey, till the end of the Second Empire. During this period he continued to write poetry and romances. Of these latter the most important is the *Misérables*. When Napoleon III., his great enemy, was defeated at Sedan, and when the Third Republic had been proclaimed, in September 1870, Hugo hastened to return to his dear Paris, and remained there to the end of his life, busy writing, and enjoying the distinction of being the most celebrated Frenchman of his time. He died on the 22nd of May 1885, and was buried in the Panthéon.

IX.

All Frenchmen are agreed that Molière is the greatest writer that France has produced. His real name was Jean Baptiste Poquelin, and he was born in Paris in 1622, although it was long supposed that he was born two years earlier. The history of his youth is somewhat obscure, but it is probable that he received a good education. It is unlikely that his father intended that his son should become a comedian; but we know that at an early age the young man resolved to adopt that profession, for, when he was but 21, he founded a company of actors called the *Illustre Théâtre*, and began to give representations in Paris. The enterprise had, however, little success, and Molière soon found himself in prison for debt. After his release, he, with his troupe, left Paris and played in a number of provincial towns during a period of some thirteen or fourteen years. In 1658, he was invited to play before the king and court in the palace of the Louvre. The king was so well pleased with the representation that Molière's troupe was put under the patronage of the king's brother, and received the right to play in Paris. The provincial life was at an end, and good fortune had come to the poor comedian. From this date, 1658, till his death in 1673, Molière continued to receive favors from the king, whilst he busied himself in writing and playing those splendid comedies which have rendered him so famous. Molière appears to have had a serious conception of the art of comedy. He reproves what is bad and encourages what is good. Among the most celebrated of his plays are: *Les Précieuses ridicules*, a satire upon the blue-stockings of his day; *Le Tartuffe*, a castigation of the religious hypocrite; *Le Misanthrope*, a satire upon the man of morose temper; and *Le Bourgeois gentilhomme*, a delightful satire on the weaknesses of the *parvenu*.

X.

Critics have regarded the essays of Montaigne as amongst the masterpieces of literature. They have been translated into all languages, and have been

admired by all for their wisdom and their clearness.
Montaigne appears to have been the first to use the
word *essai* in the sense of a short treatise. Those
written by him number 107, and in their original
form were contained in three books. They are
on a great variety of subjects: social and political
problems, religious and theological discussions, history, philosophy, and literary criticism. Montaigne is the refined, scholarly gentleman, who
sees all sides of a question, and can give all the arguments for and against any proposition. His motto is,
Que sais-je? The answer is evident: I know
nothing, and hence it becomes me to be humble and
tolerant. Montaigne was born in Périgord, in the
centre of France, in the year 1533. He was of a
good family, and great care was bestowed on his education. He learned Latin while still a child, before
he knew his mother tongue, from a German tutor
who spoke Latin. In one of his essays he speaks
with admiration of this method of learning foreign
languages. He studied law, and was appointed
magistrate in his native town, and afterwards a judge
in the *Parlement* of Bordeaux. He came to court
several times during the reigns of Henry II. and
Charles IX., and was much admired for his wit and
learning. He travelled in Germany, Switzerland and
Italy, and, on one occasion, the citizens of Rome did
him the honor of conferring on him the rights of
citizenship. At length, after a comparatively short
life, he died in 1592.

XI.

François Rabelais, the creator of those grotesque figures, Gargantua and Pantagruel, is one of the most striking characters of the period of the Renaissance. The date of his birth is not accurately known, but it was probably about 1495. His parents intended him for the ecclesiastical profession, and he studied with that end in view. He soon distinguished himself for his learning, and was made priest about 1520. He entered the order of Saint Benoît in 1524. But he soon grew weary and left the monastery without permission. Under the protection of an old friend, he then began the study of the natural sciences and medicine. Later, we find him as physician in the hospitals of Lyons, and still later, a member of the retinue of Cardinal Du Bellay, whom he twice accompanied to Rome. We then find him lecturing on medicine at Montpellier, and practising medicine at Narbonne and Lyons. His patron, the Cardinal, appointed him canon in an abbey, but he soon grew weary and resumed his wandering life. He travelled over Italy and Savoy, and returned to France, where he was protected by the King, Francis I., from the persecutions which he raised against himself by his satire of Pantagruel. After the death of Francis, we find him in Metz, where he holds the position of physician of the city. Finally, he is appointed by the Cardinal du Châtillon parish priest of Meudon, a designation which he often bears. He is supposed to have died about 1553. Gargantua and Pantagruel, father and son, are kings of a Utopia. Their lives are told by Rabelais in a grotesque and comical manner, with much satire on human affairs in general. These books belong to the same class as the celebrated "Gulliver's Travels," by the Englishman Swift.

XII.

Bossuet, who, on account of his eloquence, was called the Eagle of Meaux, is one of the glories of the reign of Louis XIV. He was born in 1627, at Dijon in the east of France. He was educated in the Jesuit college of his native town and in the *Collège de Navarre*, at Paris. At the age of 25 he was appointed to a canonry at Metz, and soon attracted attention by his eloquence as a writer and orator. In 1661, he was invited to preach before Louis XIV., in the Louvre. He remained in Paris till 1669, when he was appointed Bishop of Condom, where he remained but a short time. He then became tutor of the Dauphin, for whose instruction he wrote a Universal History. In 1680, he was elected to the Academy, and in the following year he was made Bishop of Meaux. He died in Paris in 1704, crowned with honors. Among Bossuet's most important works are his *Oraisons funèbres*, sermons preached at the burial of a number of persons of elevated rank, such as Henrietta Maria, queen of Charles I. of England; Henrietta, Duchess of Orleans, daughter of Charles;

the Prince of Condé, and others. These sermons are distinguished by lofty sentiment, vigor of thought and polished eloquence. In his *Histoire des variations des Églises protestantes*, he tries to prove that the Protestant church can not be the true church, since it is divided into so many sects. In his *Discours sur l'histoire universelle*, already referred to, his object is to prove that the whole course of human affairs shows that there is a Providence which guides all men in their actions. This latter work was one of the first attempts in modern times to construct a philosophy of history.

XIII.

Blaise Pascal is one of the most fascinating characters in the literary history of France. He was born in Auvergne in 1623, and died in Paris in 1662, at the early age of 39 years. The family was well-to-do, and possessed a taste for literature and science. So the young Pascal began early to study serious things. He was a great lover of mathematics and physics, and made important discoveries in these sciences. But he was also extremely pious, and associated himself with the most austere branch of the Catholic church in the France of his time. This was the group known as the Jansenists of Port Royal, which had a very long and bitter dispute with the Jesuits, concerning the doctrines of Grace. At the moment when victory seemed to have declared itself in favor of the Jesuits, Pascal was persuaded by the brothers of Port Royal to enter the lists. He began to write that series of memorable letters to a friend in the Provinces, under the pseudonym of Louis de Montalte, which are generally known by the name of *Les Lettres provinciales.* There were eighteen of them, and their publication extended over a period of fifteen months. In the first letters, he discussed the doctrine of Grace, but soon turned the whole force of his satire against the maxims and practices of the Jesuits, as he claimed to find these in the writings of members of that order. These letters are models of polished satire. Pascal also left to posterity a collection of short articles on pious subjects, to which the name of *Pensées* has been given. These are amongst the finest examples of epigrammatic style to be found in the French language.

XIV.

Voltaire, whose real name was Arouet, was born in Paris in 1694. He was sent at nine years of age to the *Collège Louis-le-Grand,* at that time a Jesuit school. He had a bright, active mind, and made such great progress in his studies that he delighted his masters. He early showed his taste for literature, and distinguished himself while at school by making good verses. After the death of Louis XIV., Voltaire was accused of having written a satire upon the Regent, the Duc d'Orléans, and was thrown into the Bastille, where he remained for nearly a year, occupied in composing a play and an epic poem. His epic poem had for its subject the exploits of Henry IV., and Voltaire showed in it great admiration for religious tolerance. On account of a quarrel with a nobleman, Voltaire was again put into the Bastille, and was set free on condition that he would depart for England, where he landed in May 1726. He remained in England for three years, and made the acquaintance of statesmen and literary men, and learned a good deal about English literature. His stay in England had a profound influence upon his subsequent life. He soon published his *Lettres anglaises*. These contained sentiments so distasteful to the authorities that Voltaire removed from Paris to Cirey, where he busied himself in writing plays, poetry and history, and in studying the natural sciences. In time he was restored to favor at court, and was appointed historiographer royal. At this time, a most remarkable man occupied the throne of Prussia, namely, Frederick the Great; and he invited Voltaire to reside at his court. Voltaire accepted the invitation, and spent about three years with Frederick. He passed the greater part of the remainder of his life at Ferney, near Geneva, and accordingly received the surname of the Patriarch of Ferney. Many curious stories are told of him. For instance, he had a church built at Ferney, and although he was far from being a good Catholic, the good *curé* could not prevent him from communicating, and even from preaching occasionally. He died in Paris in 1778. Voltaire's versatility was remarkable. He essayed every kind of literary composition, and excelled in all.

XV.

The date of the birth of Jacques Cartier, the discoverer of Canada, is not known with certainty. It was probably about 1491. Nor is much known regarding his early years. We know that he was a sailor, and it has been supposed that he had visited Newfoundland, and perhaps Brazil, before starting on his first voyage of discovery, which he made from Saint Malo, his native town, in 1534. After a passage of twenty days, he landed at Cape Bonavista, in Newfoundland. Leaving there, he passed by the Straits of Belle-Isle into the Gulf of St. Lawrence, saw the Magdalen Islands and landed at the Baie des Chaleurs, where he erected a cross bearing the arms of France with three *fleurs de lys* and an inscription, *Vive le Roi de France.* He then proceeded to the Bay of Gaspé and shortly afterwards returned to Saint Malo, setting sail from the port of Blanc-Sablon on the south coast of Labrador. In the following year, he set sail again from Saint Malo, and this time sailed up the St. Lawrence to Stadacona, now called Quebec, where he was received in a kindly manner by Donnacona, king of the natives. In a few weeks, Cartier proceeded up the river as far as Hochelaga, now called Montreal. He soon returned to Stadacona, and resolved to pass the winter there. He and his companions were ill prepared for the cold weather, and suffered greatly from scurvy. When spring returned he set sail for France, taking with him Donnacona and several other chiefs whom he had seized. Cartier did not return to Canada till the year 1541, when he made his third voyage. This time he ascended the river again as far as Hochelaga, and tried to pass the Sault Saint Louis, now called the Lachine rapids, but was unable to do so. He then descended the river to Stadacona, and passed the winter there. In the spring he set out for France again. It is supposed by some that he made a fourth voyage, but nothing certain is known regarding it. The date of Cartier's death is not definitely known, but it took place probably in 1557, in Saint Malo.

XVI.

Samuel de Champlain, first governor of Canada and founder of the city of Quebec, was born in 1567. He had been a seaman, and made his first voyage to Canada in 1603. He advanced as far as Hochelaga, but was unable to pass the Sault Saint Louis. From 1603 to 1607 he explored the shores of the St. Lawrence from Tadoussac to Three Rivers, giving to many places the names which they still bear. In 1608, he cleared the ground where part of the city of Quebec stands, and erected habitations. During the following years he explored the country in all directions. He ascended the Richelieu river and discovered the lake that bears his name. Later, he ascended the Ottawa river as far as Lake Nipissing and passed into Lake Huron. He then returned to Lake Simcoe and proceeded by way of the Trent river to Lake Ontario, crossing the lake to the southern side. He made a clearing also where Montreal now is, erected a fort to facilitate trading with the Indians, and called it *Place Royale*. Champlain made treaties with certain tribes of Indians who were enemies of the Iroquois, and helped them to make war on the latter. But it would have been better for the young colony if Champlain had left the Iroquois in peace. His conflicts with them were not always crowned with success. In 1629, an English fleet under the command of Sir David Kirke captured Quebec and took Champlain prisoner. But, in 1632, Quebec was restored to France by treaty, and in the following year Champlain was made first governor of Canada, or New France as it was then called. In 1635, he died at Quebec deeply regretted, and justly so. He was a good man, a man of honor and probity, and endowed with great penetration and activity.

XVII.

Louis de Buade, Comte de Frontenac, one of the most celebrated men of French Canada, was, as we see from his name, of noble origin. He was born in 1620, and when still very young entered the army and spent with distinction a number of years as soldier, rising to the rank of *maréchal de camp*. He had experience also of the life of the court, and possessed fine manners and a distinguished bearing.

In 1672, when he was fifty-two, he was sent to Quebec by Louis XIV. as governor of New France. His first period of rule extended over ten years, during which he encouraged trade with the Indians and the settlement of the country. He appears to have had a great influence over the Indians, but he did not succeed well in ruling the Frenchmen who were under him, and the king in 1682 recalled him in order to make peace. But after seven years of bad administration, Frontenac was sent again to Canada for the purpose of restoring order. During the remaining nine years of his life, he was engaged in struggling with the English colonies established in what is now part of the United States, and with their Indian allies, the fierce Iroquois. He sent out several expeditions into New England, which succeeded in burning villages and in slaying their peaceful inhabitants. The English colonists retaliated. Their most celebrated expedition was conducted by one Sir William Phips, who, with his fleet, ascended the St. Lawrence and made a feeble attack on the city of Quebec. Phips retired without success, and, before he reached Boston, lost several ships and many of his men. The Iroquois inflicted greater losses on the French. At last, in 1698, at the age of 78 years, Frontenac died at Quebec, and was buried there.

XVIII.

Early in the history of the French occupation of Canada, the Catholic church sent out priests from

France to give spiritual aid to Frenchmen, and also to preach the gospel to the savages. Champlain in 1615 brought with him four Récollet Fathers, one of whom particularly, Father Le Caron, became celebrated as a discoverer and missionary. But the most important amongst these early missionaries were the Jesuits, who arrived first in 1625. They established missions in several parts of the country, but perhaps the most celebrated were those which they established amongst the Hurons in what is now the county of Simcoe, in the province of Ontario. Here they lived with the savages for about twenty-five years, and succeeded in converting many of them to Christianity and in teaching them many of the arts of peace. But, in 1648 and 1649, these Huron settlements were attacked by their enemies the Iroquois, and a number of the brave priests met the death of martyrs. The most celebrated of these was the hero, Jean de Brébeuf, who was born in Normandy in 1593. He was a man endowed with great physical strength and great courage. He could endure all sorts of fatigue, and by his achievements in this respect, he first won the esteem of the Indians. In the month of March 1649, the fierce Iroquois, having attacked the Huron village of St. Louis, seized Brébeuf and his companion Lalemant. He was bound to a stake and was forced to endure the most horrible cruelties. His enemies tore out pieces of his flesh and ate it in his presence, and scorched him with firebrands. But he uttered no cry of pain. He tried rather to preach to them the gospel of the grace of God. They poured boiling water on his head in mockery of the sacrament of baptism. At last, in spite of his strength, he could resist no longer, and his spirit fled. His bones were taken to Quebec, and his skull may still be seen in the Hôtel-Dieu of that city.

XIX.

When Canada was a new country, two hundred years ago, the inhabitants were often forced to defend themselves with great courage against the wild beasts and the fierce Indians. Frequently it was women or young girls who won distinction by their bravery in defending themselves and their relatives. One of these brave girls was Madeleine, daughter of the Seignior of Verchères. The father was absent in Quebec and the mother in Montreal, and Madeleine was alone with her two brothers, boys of twelve and ten years, two soldiers, an old man of eighty, and some women and children. The Iroquois attacked the fort and the two soldiers ran and hid themselves. The women and children were crying; and to poor Madeleine, who was only fourteen, was left the defence of the place. She at once repaired the breaches in the palisade, and finding the two soldiers, inspired them with courage. She ordered the soldiers and her brothers to fire on the Iroquois, and she went alone to the river to meet a poor settler and his family who desired to enter the fort. The Indians, thinking that this was a ruse to draw them to the fort, did not attack her, and so she was able to accompany the settler and his family into the fort. She sent the two soldiers and the settler, with the women and children, into the blockhouse, while she remained with the old man of eighty, her two brothers and another man to protect the fort. During the night they made so much noise by crying, *Qui vive,* that the Iroquois thought the place was full of soldiers. The young girl did not eat nor sleep for days. At last, after a week, a company of forty soldiers arrived one night. As soon as Madeleine discovered who it was, she saluted the lieutenant and surrendered her arms to him. This took place in the year 1692.

XX.

François Xavier de Laval-Montmorency, the first bishop of Quebec, one of the most interesting personages in Canadian history, was born in 1623. He was of a noble family, and was heir to a great name. But from his earliest youth his aspirations were turned towards holy things. He received the tonsure at the age of nine. Later he became one of a band of young zealots, who had their head-quarters in the house of one Bernières, at Caen in Normandy. Distinguished for his piety, Laval was chosen as one fit to rule the church of New France. In 1658, the Pope created him Bishop of Petræa and Apostolic Vicar of New France, and on Easter day, 1659, he set sail for his new country. Upon his arrival he began at once to busy himself with the affairs of his charge, and before long he became the most important man in the country. In 1674, he was made Bishop of Quebec, and resigned his charge in 1685. He then proceeded to France and remained in that country for four years, although he never ceased to sigh for the privilege of returning to his old flock. On his return, he was received with great favor by the Canadians, and continued to exercise great influence till the end of his life in 1708. It was Laval who organized the clergy of Lower Canada, and he did his work well. He provided for the education of the priests by founding the Grand Séminaire and the Petit Séminaire, which still exist, and enjoy such ample revenues. He founded the system of tithes, which, although modified, also still exists. His name is held in great veneration by the people of Quebec.

XXI.

The Sorbonne is perhaps the best known of all the colleges of France. It was founded about 1256 by Robert de Sorbon, who was chaplain to Louis IX. Robert's intention was to establish a boarding-house for poor students in theology, where they might obtain good food and lodging at a moderate price, and have a quiet place for study. The house became celebrated for the serious character of its inmates, and after a certain time chairs of instruction were established. In course of time, it became celebrated also for the quality of instruction which was given, and for the severity of the examinations which it caused its students to undergo. During the Middle Ages and also in succeeding centuries, the doctors of the Sorbonne were regarded as the most learned in all matters connected with theology; and so it became common to refer disputed points to them. In the seventeenth century, the great Cardinal Richelieu, minister of Louis XIII., spent a large sum of money in the construction of new buildings for the Sorbonne; and the college continued to occupy them till the Revolution, when it was abolished, and the buildings were used as an art museum. In 1808, Napoleon reorganized the University of France, and soon after the Sorbonne was revived and became the seat of the *Académie de Paris*. A very brilliant part of its history followed, when such distinguished professors as Guizot, Cousin and Villemain filled its chairs. Since 1870 it may be said to have had another renaissance, and it is to-day one of the most important educational institutions in the world. It has just entered a splendid new edifice, erected at a cost of many millions of francs, which stands upon the site of the college built by Richelieu. The only part of the old buildings which still remains is the chapel.

PART IV.—MISCELLANEOUS PASSAGES.

1.

France is bounded on the north-west by the North Sea, the Straits of Dover and the English Channel; on the west by the Atlantic Ocean; on the south by the river Bidassoa, the Pyrenees and the Mediterranean; on the east by the Alps, which separate it from Italy, by the Lake of Geneva, the Jura Mountains, which separate it from Switzerland, and by the Vosges Mountains, which separate it from Germany; and on the north-east and north by a conventional line which separates it from Germany, the Grand-Duchy of Luxembourg and Belgium. France comprises also some small islands scattered along the coast and one large island, Corsica, situated in the Mediterranean, 160 kilometres to the south of the French coast. The present area of France is about 528,000 square kilometres, representing almost the thousandth part of the area of the globe, or the nineteenth part of that of Europe. Its greatest length, from north to south, is 1000 kilometres, and its greatest width, from east to west, is about 960 kilometres. France is the only country which touches at one and the same time the Mediterranean, the Atlantic, and the North Sea. It possesses all varieties of climate and soil, and borders on five of the richest States of

Continental Europe—Belgium, Germany, Switzerland, Italy and Spain—and is separated from England by a strait only. Hence it seems that nature has prepared it to play a great part amongst the other nations in commerce as well as in politics.

II.

Frenchmen call France the most beautiful country in the world. It is also a country rich in natural products. Owing to the variety of soil and climate the number of products is very varied. The most important cereals are wheat, rye, oats, barley and Indian corn, of which many millions of bushels are grown. Of these wheat is the most important, and the richest regions of wheat culture are in the north, north-east and central parts of the country. Besides the cereals there are other plants which furnish great wealth to the people of France, as, for example, potatoes, an important article of food; sugar-beets, from which are made large quantities of sugar; flax, from which linen is made, and tobacco. The meadows of France are of great extent and richness. Those of Normandy and Brittany are particularly celebrated. On these great herds of cattle feed, from which come the beef, milk and butter which have made these parts of France famous. France is rich also in fruits. Apples, pears, cherries, and the like, abound in the northern parts; whilst figs, peaches, apricots, oranges and lemons grow in the south. But the most important of all French fruits is the grape. It grows in all parts of the country, but certain localities are more famous than others. For instance, the vineyards of the banks of the Rhone, those of Burgundy and Champagne in the east of France, as well as those in the districts surrounding Angoulême and Bordeaux in the west, are very celebrated. Unfortunately the vines of France have suffered greatly during late years from a number of diseases, the most destructive of which is the *phylloxéra*, against which no complete remedy has yet been found.

III.

Amongst the cultivated trees of France the first rank belongs to the mulberry, on account of the fact that the silk-worm feeds upon the leaves of this tree. It is in the departments bordering on the lower Rhone that we find the greatest development of silk culture, that is to say, in the warm part of France; for neither mulberries nor silk-worms thrive in cold climates. Lyons, situated on the Rhone, is the chief seat of the manufacture of silk in France. Besides apple-trees, pear-trees, cherry-trees and the like, there are other fruit-trees which play an important part in the domestic economy of the people. Such are the chestnut-tree, which grows on the mountain sides in the south of France, and which gives food to large numbers of people where cereals and potatoes are cultivated with difficulty, and the olive-tree, whose fruit gives the oil which is an important article of food in the warmer parts of Europe, where butter can not be made and kept so easily as where the weather is cool. The forests of France are of considerable importance also, for coal is much more rare there than in England. The oak is the most important of the forest trees of France, both on account of its wide distribution and of its value in commerce. It furnishes building timber, firewood and tan-bark. The elm and beech grow in all parts of the country and are used as firewood, and in various trades, such as joiner work and carriage building. The ash, sycamore and poplar are also common and are used in carpenter and cabinet work. Amongst evergreen trees the various kinds of the pine are the most important, for they are very hardy, and very useful in all sorts of industry. A very interesting tree is the cork-oak, whose bark furnishes the material out of which corks and many other articles are made. In France it is found only in the south. Other trees, such as the horse-chestnut and the linden tree, are rather to be considered as ornamental trees.

IV.

Paris, the capital of France, is one of the great cities of the world. It is situated on both sides of the Seine, at about forty-nine degrees north latitude. As it is the seat of the central government, we find in it the various departments of the public administration, —the Senate, the Chamber of Deputies, and the Law Courts. It is also the seat of the great financial institutions, such as the Bank of France, the centre of the railways and of the telegraph system, and the home of many important industries, such as manufactures of clothing, furniture, goldsmith's work and jewelry, printing and engraving, musical and scientific instruments, chemical products, etc. Paris is celebrated for its splendid public buildings, amongst which are the Louvre, once a royal palace, now a museum of antiquities and an art gallery, the Luxembourg, once the residence of Marie de Médicis, now the seat of the Senate, and the Palais de Justice, the seat of the courts of law; there are also the celebrated churches of Notre-Dame de Paris, the Sainte-Chapelle, the Panthéon and the Madeleine. Paris is renowned also for its schools and colleges, the most celebrated of which are the Sorbonne, the Collège de France, and the École de Médecine, in which the most eminent scholars of the world have been and are professors. Paris is above all the home of the fine arts. Its museums and galleries are amongst the finest in the world, and thousands of artists from all parts of the world gather in its studios. Its theatres and operas are organized on a grand scale, and no city in the world has more distinguished dramatic authors, composers and actors.

v.

There is a magnificent square in Paris, on the right bank of the Seine, called the Place de la Concorde, around which rise eight colossal statues of female figures representing the chief cities of France. Let us talk a little of these cities. LILLE, in the north-eastern part of France near Belgium, is situated in a fertile locality and has important manufactures of linen, cotton, beet-root sugar, chemical products and steam-engines. ROUEN is situated on the Seine at about eighty miles from its mouth, and, although at so great a distance from the sea, is the fourth port in France. It has a large commerce and manufactures of cotton, wool and silk. It is also very celebrated for its public buildings, particularly its cathedral, which dates from the thirteenth century. LYON, on the banks of the Rhone, is renowned as the centre of the silk industries. It is the second city in France in point of population. MARSEILLE is one of the oldest cities in France, having been founded by the Greeks centuries before the Christian era. It is the most important seaport of the Mediterranean, and is the third city in France in point of population. Besides its commerce, which exceeds two billions and a half annually, Marseille is celebrated for its manufactures of soap, candles, matches and steam-engines. BORDEAUX, the third seaport of France, is situated on the left bank of the Garonne. It is the centre of an important wine district and is celebrated for its exports of wine and brandy. Its chief industries are vinegar, sugar, woollen goods, paper, earthenware, and glassware. It is also celebrated for its colleges and museums. NANTES, situated on the right bank of the Loire, is one of the greatest French seaports, and a centre for sugar refining, for preparing canned provisions, particularly the sardine, for ship-building and for agricultural machines. BREST, at the northwest corner of France in Finistère, is a fortified seaport celebrated for its fine harbor and extensive drydocks and ship-yards. STRASBOURG is the last of the eight cities represented by the statues of the Place de la Concorde. It is no longer a French city, having been ceded to Germany after the war of 1870. It is the capital of Alsace and is situated on the Rhine. Its commerce is important. Its chief manufactures are machinery and watches. It is celebrated for its beautiful cathedral and for a well-equipped university. The loss of Strasbourg was a source of great sorrow to the French. Every year on the fourteenth of July, the national holiday, the patriotic societies of Paris hang the statue of Strasbourg with garlands, and make touching speeches in front of it.

VI.

In the large towns of France, and especially in Paris, the inhabitants are not spread over so large an extent of ground as they are in England and Canada. Indeed, one may say that there are nearly everywhere in Paris five layers of people, and often seven. That implies that the houses have from five to eight stories. Hence it is that the city is so compact, although it is the most populous in Europe after London. The streets are formed by high houses on both sides, very uniform in appearance, so that their regularity becomes a little monotonous. We shall now visit a Parisian house, and you will be kind enough to remark the peculiarities of its arrangement.

In the first place, a Parisian house is often so very like its neighbors on both sides, and so closely joined to them, that one has a little difficulty in distinguishing it from them. On looking at it, you see a high building with many windows, and the main door in the middle, on a level with the foot-pavement or sidewalk. It is this door that is numbered; and the shops that are often seen, one on each side of it, are both known by the same number. These shops usually have their own doors, but they do not count in numbering the houses. The main door, then, is very wide and high, and often has two leaves. It closes the outer extremity of an archway which completely pierces the part of the building that fronts on the street, and it is made wide enough to allow a carriage or a cart to go in, because it forms the only entrance to the court which is behind. On going through this archway we enter the court, and you will see that it is enclosed on three sides, and often on four, by the front, wings and rear block of the building, which thus forms a quadrangle with the court in the centre. Raising your eyes to these high walls, you may count as many as a hundred windows looking down at you.

Now, to discover who live in this enormous house, let us retrace our steps to the outer door. The first person we remark is the porter, or the "concierge," as he prefers to be called now-a-days. He has seen us pass the door of his lodge, which is on one side of the archway, and he has come out to know what we want. We ought to have spoken to him as we passed his door, for that is the rule. He is the guardian of the whole house, and lets no stranger pass without asking him his business. You see he has a glass door opening on the archway; and beside his chair there is a little window known by the curious name of *vasistas*, and serving to speak to people who are passing. You see, too, a cord with a tassel or a ring at the end of it, hanging where he usually sits. I must explain to you what that is for. If you come to the door after dark, you will find it shut. You pull the bell. At once you hear the bolt drawn back and the door opens of itself. You step in and shut it behind you, for you see nobody. The cord there in the lodge enables the concierge to pull the bolt without moving from his place. If, on the other hand, you come down stairs to go out at any time after the door is shut, or before it is open in the morning, you call out to the concierge, "Cord, if you please!" and the door opens at once. You must know he has another cord hanging at the head of his bed, which he pulls to open the door for those who come in late or go out very early.

Now come a little farther in the direction of the court, and you will find the stairway leading to the upper stories. At the foot of the stair there is often a hall, generally rather small. In front of the first step of the stair there is a large mat, and on the balusters often hangs a notice on pasteboard, with the words, "Wipe your feet, S. V. P."

As soon as you begin to climb the stair, you find that the concierge has waxed and polished the steps so well that you would sometimes slip if you did not hold by the hand-rail. As you may imagine, it is still more dangerous when one runs down the stair rapidly.

But here we are on the landing. In the old houses this story is low and is called the *entresol*, the next above being the first floor. As the *entresol* has the same arrangement of rooms as the rest of the floors, and as the vacant suite of apartments we are going to look at is on the third, we shall go on. You have already noticed that on each landing there are two doors with bell-pulls beside them. Each of these doors opens into a series of rooms, which are entirely cut off from the rest of the house, and are intended to form a family dwelling. That is the way people live in French cities, the rich as well as the poor.

At last we are arrived at the third floor, which is, properly speaking, the fourth. The concierge will now open the door and show us the rooms. We first enter the ante-chamber, then we see a passage leading straight forward, or the ante-chamber and passage may be in one. On one side you will find the kitchen and pantry; on the other you see the dining-room and drawing-room and then a bedroom or two, and so on, according to the size of the house. In short, you will find here almost everything to make a whole family comfortable. I must tell you, however, that each set of apartments has its own division of the great cellar which is under the house, and there people keep the coals, wood and wine, when they buy large supplies of these commodities.

VII.

The parts of the harness of a horse are as follows. The bridle is fitted to his head and carries the bit which is placed in his mouth, as well as the blinkers to cover his eyes. To the bit are attached the reins and also the bearing-rein. On the neck is placed the collar, upon which are fitted the hames which carry one end of the traces. There are other parts of the harness, such as the saddle and girth, the crupper, the breeching and other parts of less importance. Every one should know these names, and should learn how to harness and unharness a horse, as well as how to put him into a carriage and drive him without danger.

It is well to know how to ride, too. For that you need a saddle and a bridle, and sometimes spurs and riding-whip. Your feet rest in the stirrups, and you soon learn how to keep your equilibrium under ordinary circumstances.

VIII.

What are the principal parts of a four-wheeled carriage? Let us begin with the front. If it is a one-horse carriage, we see the shafts, between which the horse is placed; if it is a two-horse carriage, instead of the shafts we find a pole. Then we see the whiffle-tree, to which the traces are fastened. This is connected more or less directly with the axle of the fore wheels, and the latter with the axle of the hind wheels. Each wheel is composed of the hub, the spokes, the rim, which is made up of pieces of wood called the felloes, and lastly the outer iron rim called the tire, which is sometimes covered with India-rubber, like a bicycle wheel. To lessen the jolting which is produced in passing over a rough road, the carriage is provided with springs before and behind, and the seats are covered with cushions. The body of the carriage rests on the springs. It may be of different shapes, it may be open or closed, it may have seats for two or four or six, and perhaps places for a coachman and a footman. If it is a covered carriage—a brougham, for instance—it has on each side a door containing in the upper half a window over which a blind may be drawn. Below the door there is a step, on which people put their feet in getting in and out. Some carriages have also splash-boards over the wheels to keep the mud from flying up when they run fast.

IX.

In France, when people wish to be carried from one place to another, and don't want to call a cab, they take an omnibus or tram-car. Paris has a service of thirty-four omnibus lines and about fifty tram lines. The omnibuses take the winding routes, and the tramways are laid down along the straighter and more important streets.

The lighter omnibuses are drawn by two horses, and the heavier ones, which carry as many as forty passengers, are drawn by three horses driven abreast. The tram-cars have usually only two horses, but they carry from sixty to seventy passengers. The number of passengers carried by each omnibus or tram-car is limited by the number of seats plus the space on the rear platform. When all of these regular places are filled, the conductor will allow no more passengers to get on. That is the law, and it is never violated. To show that his omnibus or tram-car is filled, the conductor exposes to view a small sign with the word "*complet*" on it. When you see that word it is useless to try to get into the vehicle that carries it.

To get into an omnibus or tram-car is at any time quite a business. You are not allowed to get in anywhere you like, unless you are at some distance from the regular stopping-place. You generally go to the nearest station and wait for your omnibus to come. But that is not enough. When you enter the waiting-room, you go up to the counter and name the line you wish to take. The man who sits behind the counter gives you a round ticket with a number on it. If it is number one, you have the first claim to a seat in the first omnibus that arrives on the line indicated by the color of the ticket. You wait till the *contrôleur* calls out the name of your line. Then you go out and take your place behind the omnibus and listen to the numbers called out. When you hear yours, you step forward, give up your number and take your place. As soon as all the places are filled, or all the numbers exhausted, the omnibus drives on. If you happen to have a high number, or the omnibus arrives already filled, you may have to wait for some time.

Most omnibuses and tram-cars carry passengers both outside and in. The outside places are on the rear platform, where you have to stand, and on the top, where the seats are arranged lengthwise, as they are inside. The top is called in France the *impériale*. The fare for the top is fifteen centimes or three sous; and for the inside, thirty centimes or six sous. You pay your fare directly to the conductor, for there are no tickets for the ordinary passenger. The conductor must mark the entrance of each person by pulling a cord attached to a sort of register, which shows how many have got in, and which has a bell that rings when the cord is pulled. At each stopping-place there is a man who, among other things, watches that the number of passengers is correctly recorded on the register.

The inside passengers and those who stand on the platform are entitled to transfer-tickets free, those on the top can obtain them by paying fifteen centimes **extra**. These tickets are called *correspondances* and give the right to take a second line. To do this, you get out at the proper station, and when your omnibus comes you give up your ticket along with your number at the door of the omnibus.

The man who drives the omnibus or tram-car is called the *cocher*, the man who takes the fares is the *conducteur*, and the man who stands at the station to oversee what goes on is called, as we have seen above, the *contrôleur*.

Most of the omnibuses and tram-cars in Paris are still drawn by horses. But there are a few tram lines which go by steam, electricity or compressed air. The electricity is supplied by means of accumulators and not through conducting wires. Indeed there are no wires visible in Paris, not even the telephone wires; all are under ground

---

A certain Englishman not very well up in French, came home from France and complained that there was a place in Paris that he had not been able to visit. He saw a number of omnibuses and tramcars evidently going to a place called Complet; but in spite of all his efforts, the conductors would never allow him to get on. He called to them in vain; they paid no heed to him; and that is why he never saw Complet.

X.

There are farms in Lower Canada, on the banks of the St. Lawrence below Quebec, which are only ninety yards—or, as the *habitant* says, an acre and a half—wide, and a league and a half long. They are of this peculiar shape because everybody wishes to have on his own farm all the sorts of land which exist in the locality. Every farmer wishes to have a piece of land which is covered with water when the tide is high, where he may cut coarse hay for his cows in winter; he wishes a piece of drier land, clay or light soil, on which he may raise his oats, wheat, peas or flax; and he wishes a piece of the mountain, where he may cut wood in winter and where he may make his maple sugar in spring. The Lower Canadian farmer's manner of living is simple but extremely interesting. There are many things of which he is ignorant—often fortunately for him—but he is very expert in making use of the resources which nature offers him. He strips the hemlock and oak of their bark, and tans his own leather, of which he makes boots for himself and harness for his horses. Not only do his wife and daughters card, spin and weave the wool which his sheep produce, but even the flax which he raises is turned by their clever hands into good linen cloth, from which are made sacks for holding grain, and sometimes sheets for beds. The *habitant* frequently makes his own farm implements, such as rakes and harrows, and sometimes even ploughs and carts. Thus it is easy to see that he leads a very independent life. If the good Lord sends him rain and sunshine, he smiles, sings his beautiful, simple songs, pays his tithes and fears no man.

XI.

Let us talk about the trees of Canada. Respecting the majority of these trees English Canadians use the same names as Englishmen, and French Canadians use the same names as Frenchmen. But there are a few for which we of this country have names different from those which one hears in Europe. We shall prefer the former in case of difference. Let us begin with the maple, whose leaf has been chosen as our national emblem. There are several varieties of the maple, but the one we love the most is the sugar-maple which does not grow in Europe, but which is very abundant in our country. It is a very beautiful tree, particularly in autumn, after its leaves begin to change color. Its wood is strong and hard, and is capable of being highly polished, and consequently is much esteemed by carpenters, cabinet-makers and carriage-builders. The beech is another beautiful and useful tree which is much like the European variety. It bears a fruit, the beech-nut, which is much esteemed by Canadian boys, as well as by squirrels. The elm, the oak, the ash, the basswood, and many other deciduous trees, are abundant in our forests, and are used either as firewood or in the manufacture of many sorts of tools and machines, or in the building of ships, houses and railway carriages. The conifers, most of which are evergreen, are also very abundant amongst us. The most important representative of this family is the pine, whose stately form is a striking figure in all our forests. Our pine woods are amongst the richest resources of our country. It is the pine which absorbs almost completely the activity of our lumber shanties, and which furnishes a great part of our lumber trade. The hemlock is another useful tree, although less esteemed than the pine. The spruce, balsam and tamarac are also valuable trees when they grow in the woods, and are frequently planted in the parks and gardens of towns and cities, which they adorn by their graceful forms and their dark foliage. Nature has, indeed, been very kind to us, but we have wasted her gifts. We have cut and burned the full-grown trees of our forests as if we were destroying enemies, and we have neglected so much to care for the young trees that we all suffer from the lack of trees to protect us and our land from the inclemencies of the climate. Every child ought to be taught to love trees and to take care of them, and the government ought to establish schools of forestry where men may be instructed in all that pertains to the care of forests, so that, some day, we may begin to replant our woods and to cover again with trees many a hill and plain which are now nothing but barren wastes.

VOCABULARY.

ABBREVIATIONS.

adj.—adjective.
adv.—adverb.
Amer.—America.
bef.—before.
conj.—conjunction.
eccl., ecclesiast.—ecclesiastical.
esp.—especially.
famil.—familiarly.
f., fem.—feminine.
fig.—figuratively.
gram.—grammar.
'h—h aspirate.
impf.—imperfect.
indic.—indicative.
inf., infin.—infinitive.
interrog.—interrogative.
lit.—literally.
m., masc.—masculine.
med.—medical.
mil., milit.—military.
m.s.—masculine singular.

n.—noun.
nav.—naval.
neg.—negative.
obj.—object.
p.—page.
p.p.—past participle.
pers.—person.
pl., plur.—plural.
pop.—popular.
prep.—preposition.
pro., pron.—pronoun.
pron.—pronounce.
qch.—quelque chose.
qn.—quelqu'un.
rel.—relative.
sing.—singular.
subj., subjunct.—subjunctive.
trans.—translate.
v.—verb.
v.a.—verb active.
v.n.—verb neuter.

VOCABULARY.

A.

a, an, un, une; *five cents a yard,* cinq sous le mètre; *five francs a day,* cinq francs par jour.
abandon, abandonner, quitter, céder.
abbey, abbaye, f.
abdicate, abdiquer.
abjure, abjurer.
able, habile, capable; à même de, en état de; *to be able to,* pouvoir; *for not being able to,* pour ne pas pouvoir.
abolish, abolir, détruire.
abound, abonder, être abondant.
about, de, près de, à peu près, autour (de), auprès de, sur, à l'égard de, touchant, environ, vers; *to be about to,* être sur le point de, aller; *to go about it,* s'y mettre; *about twelve,* environ douze; *about 1812,* vers 1812.
above, au-dessus (de); *above all,* surtout; (already mentioned) ci-dessus, déjà.
abreast, de front.
abruptly, brusquement, avec précipitation.
absence, absence, f.
absent, absent.
absolute, absolu.
absorb, absorber; *to become absorbed in,* être absorbé dans.
abstraction, abstraction, f.
abundant, abondant.
abuse, abus, m.
academy, académie, f.
accept, accepter, agréer.
accident, accident, m.; *by accident,* par hasard.
accompany (by), accompagner (de).
accomplishments, arts d'agrément, m. pl.
according to, selon, suivant.
accordingly, par conséquent, ainsi.
accost, aborder, accoster.
account, compte, m.; *on account of,* à cause de, au sujet de.
accumulator, accumulateur, m.
accurately, exactement.
accuse, accuser.
accustomed, be, être accoutumé (à), avoir coutume (de).
ache, faire mal (à); *my arms ache,* les bras me font mal.
achievement, exploit, m.
acknowledge, avouer, reconnaître, convenir.
acorn, gland, m.
acquaintance, connaissance, f., ami, m.
acquire, acquérir, obtenir.
acre, (Lower Canada) arpent, m., (France) hectare (about 2½ acres), m.
across, à travers, au travers de; *to go across,* traverser; *to come across,* rencontrer; *to rush across,* traverser en courant.
act, n., acte, m., action, f.
act, v., agir, se conduire, faire, représenter; *to act a part,* jouer un rôle.
action, action, f.
active, actif, -ve, agile.
activity, activité, f.
actor, acteur.
A.D., après Jésus-Christ, de notre ère.

add, ajouter, joindre.
address, n., adresse, f.
address, v., s'adresser à, parler à, adresser la parole à.
adieu, adieu, je vous salue.
administrate, administrer, régir.
administration, administration, f.
admiral, amiral.
admiration, admiration, f.
admire, admirer; *admired by*, admiré de.
admit, admettre, avouer.
adopt, adopter.
adorn, orner, parer.
advance, s'avancer, avancer.
advantage, avantage, m.; *to take undue advantage of*, abuser de.
advertisement, annonce, f.
advise, conseiller; *to advise him to go*, lui conseiller d'aller.
Æsop, Ésope.
affair, affaire, f.
affection, affection, f.
affirm, affirmer.
afflict, affliger.
afraid, be, avoir peur; *to be so much afraid*, avoir tellement peur (de).
Africa, Afrique, f.
after, prep. and adv., après, plus tard (*after* with pres. part. is translated by *après* with perf. part.); conj., après que.
afterwards, ensuite, plus tard, après.
again, encore, encore une fois, de nouveau; *never again*, ne...jamais plus.
against, contre; *against it*, y.
age, âge, m.; *to be four years of age*, avoir quatre ans, être âgé de quatre ans; *at the age of four*, à l'âge de quatre ans.
ago, il y a; *a moment ago*, il y a un moment.
agreed, be, convenir, être d'accord.
agricultural, agricole.
agriculture, agriculture, f.
aid, n., secours, m.

aid, v., aider (à with Inf.)
aide-de-camp, aide de camp, m.
ailment, maladie, f., mal, m., incommodité, f.
air, air, m.
Alemanni, Alemanni, Allemands, m. pl.
alike, pareil; *to be alike*, se ressembler.
alive, vif, -ve, vivant.
all, tout, tous; *all men*, tous les hommes; *all night*, toute la nuit; *at all*, du tout; *all I have*, tout ce que j'ai; adv., tout, tout à fait, fort, entièrement.
allegiance, fidélité, f.
allow, permettre (à with person, de with verb), laisser; *he was allowed to do so*, on le laissa faire, on le lui permit; *allowed himself to be crowned*, se laissa couronner.
ally, allié.
almost, presque, à peu près.
alms, aumône, f.
alone, seul.
along, le long de; dans, par; *to walk along*, se promener dans (par); *along with*, avec.
aloud, à haute voix.
alphabet, alphabet, m.
Alps, Alpes, f. pl.
already, déjà.
Alsace, f.
also, aussi, également.
although, bien que, quoique.
altogether, tout à fait, entièrement.
always, toujours.
amazement, étonnement, m.; *in amazement*, étonné.
ambassador, ambassadeur, m.
ambulance, ambulance, f.; *ambulance-waggon*, voiture d'ambulance, f.
America, Amérique, f.
American, américain.
among, amongst, entre, parmi, avec, au milieu de.
ample, ample, large.

amusing, amusant.
anarchism, anarchisme, m.
anarchist, anarchiste.
anchor, ancre, f.
ancient, vieux, vieille, ancien, antique.
and, et.
Andrew, André.
anecdote, anecdote, f.
angelus, angélus, m.
angry, fâché, en colère, irrité.
animal, animal, m.
annoy, contrarier ; *annoyed at,* contrarié de.
annually, par an, tous les ans.
another, un autre, encore un, un deuxième.
answer, n., réponse, f.
answer, v., répondre, répliquer.
ante-chamber, antichambre, f.
antiquity, antiquité, f.
anxious to, be, tenir à.
any, quelque, tout, des, de, en ; n'importe quel ; *not any greater,* pas plus grand ; *at any other time,* à toute autre heure.
anybody, quelqu'un, (with neg.) personne.
anything, quelque chose, m. (with neg.) rien.
anywhere, quelque part ; *not.... anywhere,* ne....nulle part ; *anywhere you like,* n'importe où, où vous voudrez.
apartment, chambre, f. ; *suite of apartments,* appartement, m.
apology, apologie, f., excuse, f. ; *apology for,* apologie de.
apostle, apôtre.
apostolic, apostolique.
apparently, en apparence, apparemment.
appear, paraître ; (before a court) comparaître.
appearance, apparence, f., air, m.
appetite, appétit, m.
apple, pomme, f.
apple-tree, pommier, m.
apply, s'adresser.

appoint, nommer, désigner.
apprehension, appréhension, f., crainte, f.
approach, approcher (de), s'approcher (de), aborder.
approbation, approbation, f.
apricot, abricot, m.
Arab, arabe.
arbiter, arbitre, m.
arbitrary, arbitraire.
archbishop, archevêque.
archway, voûte, f.
Arcola, Arcole, f.
area, superficie, f.
argument, argument, m.
arm, bras, m.
arms, armes, f. pl. ; *companion in arms,* compagnon d'armes.
army, armée, f.
around, autour (de).
arrange, arranger, disposer.
arrangement, arrangement, m., disposition, f.
arrival, arrivée, f. ; *upon his arrival,* à son arrivée.
arrive, arriver, parvenir.
arsenic, arsenic, m.
art, art, m.
article, article, m., objet, m.
artist, artiste, m. and f.
artless, naïf, -ve, simple, ingénu.
as, comme, puisque ; *as....as,* aussi ...que ; *as soon as,* aussitôt que ; *as well as,* aussi bien que, du mieux que.
ascend, monter.
ascribe, attribuer.
ash, frêne, m.
ask, demander (indirect object of person, *de* with verb), prier (direct object of person, *de* with verb) ; *I ask him why,* je lui demande pourquoi ; *to ask one for something,* demander quelque chose à quelqu'un ; *to ask a question of,* demander une question à, faire une question à.
asleep, endormi.
aspiration, aspiration, f.

ass, âne, m.
assassin, assassin, m.
assert, prétendre, affirmer.
associate, associer; s'associer; *to associate oneself with*, s'associer avec.
assume, prendre (sur soi), se permettre.
assure, assurer.
astonish, étonner; *astonished at*, étonné de.
astonishment, étonnement, m.
asylum, maison d'aliénés, f.
at, à, de, dans, en; *at once*, tout de suite; *at home*, chez soi, chez lui, etc.; *to laugh at*, se moquer de.
Atlantic, adj., atlantique; (of ships) transatlantique; n., Atlantique, f.
attach, attacher, lier.
attack, n., attaque, f.
attack, v.a., attaquer.
attempt, essai, m., effort, m.
attend, soigner; *to get it attended to*, le faire soigner.
attendance, présence, f., assistance, f.
attendants, suite, f.
attention, attention, f.
attract, attirer.
attribute, attribuer; *to attribute to oneself*, s'attribuer.
august, auguste.
austere, austère.
Austria, Autriche, f.
Austrian, autrichien.
author, auteur, m.
authority, autorité, f.
autumn, automne, m.; *in autumn*, en automne.
avaricious, avare, avaricieux.
avenge himself, se venger.
average, moyen; *on an average*, en moyenne.
avidity, avidité, f.
await, attendre.
awake, éveiller, réveiller.
awakening, réveil, m.
away with you!, allez-vous-en!
axe, hache, f.
axle, essieu, m.

B.

back, dos, m.
bad, mauvais, méchant.
badly, mal.
bag, sac, m.
bake, v.n., cuire; v.a., faire cuire, cuire.
ball, (cannon) boulet, m.
balsam, (Lower Canada) sapin, m.
balusters, rampe, f.
band, société, f., bande, f.
banish, bannir, exiler.
bank, bord, m., rive, f.; (financial) banque, f.; *on the left bank*, sur la rive gauche.
banker, banquier, m.
baptise, baptiser.
baptism, baptême, m.
bark, n., écorce, f.
bark, v., aboyer.
barley, orge, f.
barren, stérile.
base, baser, fonder.
basket, panier, m., corbeille, f.
basswood, tilleul, m., (Lower Canada) bois blanc.
Bastille, f.
bath, bain, m.; *to have a bath*, se baigner.
bathe, v.n., se baigner.
battle, bataille, f.; *battle-field*, champ de bataille, m.
bawl, crier fort.
bay, baie, f.
be, être, devoir, valoir, se trouver; *he is running*, il court; *than I am*, que moi; *to be four years old*, avoir quatre ans; *if it were not for*, si ce n'était, sans; *how is this?*, comment cela se fait-il?; *he is to go to-morrow*, il doit partir demain; *to be well*, aller bien, se porter bien; *isn't it?*, n'est-ce pas?; *to be better*, valoir mieux; *is to be found*, est à trouver, doit

VOCABULARY. 121

se trouver, peut se trouver; *it is considered (as)*, on le regarde comme; *we are arrived*, nous voilà arrivés; *it may be drawn*, on peut le tirer.
beach, plage, f.
bear, porter, supporter, endurer.
bearing, port, m.
bearing-rein, fausse rêne.
beast, bête, f., animal, m.
beat, battre, vaincre; (in speed) battre, dépasser.
beautiful, beau, magnifique.
because, parce que, de ce que.
beckon, faire signe à.
become, devenir, se faire; seoir (à with person, de with verb); *what has become of her?*, qu'est-elle devenue?
bed, lit, m.
bedroom, chambre à coucher, f.
bee, abeille, f.
beech, 'hêtre, m.
beech-nut, faîne, f.
beef, bœuf, m.
beet-root, betterave, f.
before, adv. and prep., avant (de), auparavant, autrefois; (of space) devant; *the day before*, la veille; conj., avant que.
beg, mendier; prier, demander.
beggar, mendiant.
begin, commencer (à before inf.); *to begin with*, commencer par.
beginning, commencement, m.
behave, se conduire; affecter les allures.
behind, derrière; *to leave behind*, laisser.
behold, voici, voyez.
Belgium, Belgique, f.
believe, croire; *I believe so*, je le crois, je crois que oui.
bell, sonnette, f., timbre, m.
bell-pull, cordon de sonnette, m.
belong, appartenir à, être à.
below, adv., en bas; prep., au-dessous de, plus bas que.
bench, banc, m.

bend, plier, courber; *to bend down*, se baisser.
berth, lit, m.
beseech, prier, supplier, implorer.
beside, près de, à côté de; *beside them* (of things), à côté.
besides, outre, hors (de).
besiege, assiéger.
best, le meilleur.
bestow, donner; *great care was bestowed on*, on donna les plus grands soins à.
better, adj., meilleur; adv. mieux; *you had better*, vous feriez bien (mieux) de; *to be better*, être mieux, valoir mieux.
between, entre.
beware, se méfier (de), prendre garde (à).
Bible, Bible, f.
bicycle, bicycle, m., bicyclette, f.
big, grand, gros.
billion, billion, m., milliard, m.
bind, lier, attacher.
birth, naissance, f.
birth-day, fête, f., jour de naissance, m.
biscuit, biscuit, m.
bishop, évêque.
bit, morceau, m., brin, m., (bridle) mors, m.
bite, n., morsure, f.; p. 54, use *mordu*, p.p.
bite, v., mordre.
bitter, amer, aigre, (struggle) acharné.
black, noir.
blacksmith, forgeron, m.; *blacksmith's shop*, forge, f.
bleed, saigner; *his nose bleeds*, le nez lui saigne, il saigne du nez.
blind, adj., aveugle; *blind man*, aveugle.
blind, n., store, m.
blinker, œillère, f.
block, corps (de bâtiment), m.
blockhouse, blockhaus, m.
blood, sang, m.
blot, tache, f.

blow, souffler, faire du vent, venter.
blue-stocking, bas bleu, m.
bluish, bleuâtre.
blush (with) rougir (de).
board, planche, f.; *on board*, sur, à bord (de).
boarding-house, pension, f.
body, corps, m.
body-guard, garde du corps, f.
bohemian, bohémien.
boil, bouillir.
boiling, bouillant.
bolt, verrou, m.
bomb, bombe, f.
bonds, obligations, f. pl.
bone, os, m.; (dead) *bones*, os, ossements, m. pl.
book, livre, m.
boot, (long) botte, f.; (short) bottine, f.
Bordeaux, m.
border on, confiner (à, avec), être limitrophe de; border.
born, be, naître; *was born*, naquit, était né, (of person still living) est né.
borrow of, emprunter à.
both, l'un et l'autre, tous (les) deux; *both....and*, et....et, aussi bien... que.
bottle, bouteille, f.
bottom, fond, m., bas, m.
bound, borner.
bow, révérence, f., salut, m.
box, boîte, f., (theatre) loge, f.
boy, garçon, enfant, jeune homme; *(garçon* is much less frequently used than *boy)*; *the last boy in the class*, le dernier élève, or le dernier.
boyhood, enfance, f., première jeunesse, f.
brains, cervelle, f.
bran, son, m.
branch, branche, f.
brandy, eau-de-vie, f., cognac, m.
brave, brave, courageux.
bravery, courage, m.

Brazil, Brésil, m.
breach, brèche, f.
bread, pain, m.
break, casser, briser, rompre; *to break one's neck*, se casser le cou: *to break out*, éclater.
breakfast, déjeuner, m.
breast, poitrine, f.
breath, haleine, f.
bred, élevé.
breeching, avaloire, f.
Brest, m.
bridle, bride, f.
brigand, brigand, m.
bright, vif, -ve, brillant.
brilliant, brillant.
bring, (of what one carries) apporter, (of what one conducts) amener, porter; *to bring back*, rapporter.
Brittany, Bretagne, f.; *from Brittany*, Breton.
brood over, méditer sur, rêver à.
brother, frère.
brougham, brougham, m.
Brumaire, Brumaire, m. (one of the autumn months of the Republican year).
Budæus, Budé.
build, bâtir, construire, faire bâtir.
building, n., bâtiment, m., édifice, m., monument, m., (making) construction, f.; adj., de construction.
bull, taureau, m.
bullet, balle, f.
burden, fardeau, m.
Burgundy, Bourgogne, f.
burial, enterrement, m.
burn, brûler.
burst, éclater; *to burst into a fit of laughter*, éclater de rire; *to burst out*, s'écrier.
bury, enterrer, ensevelir.
bushel, boisseau, m. (hectolitre, m., equal to 2¾ bushels, is the term always used in France to-day, in speaking of cereals).
business, affaire, affaires, f.; *one's business*, ce qu'on désire.

busy oneself with, s'occuper (de or à).
busy, occupé, affairé, agité; *busy making,* occupé à faire.
but, mais, excepté, si ce n'est que, ne...que; *nothing but,* rien que; *I have but one,* je n'en ai qu'un.
butter, beurre, m.
buy, acheter.
buzz, bourdonner.
by, par, de, à cause de, en; *by the by,* à propos; *by my watch,* à ma montre; *to pass by a house,* passer devant une maison; *by founding,* en fondant.

C.

cab, fiacre, m., voiture, f.
cabin, cabine, f., (of captain) cajute, f.
cabinet, cabinet, m.
cabinet-maker, ébéniste, m.
cabinet work, ébénisterie, f.
call, appeler, nommer; *to be called,* s'appeler, se nommer; *to call together,* assembler; *to call in,* appeler; *to call attention to,* appeler l'attention sur; *to call out of,* appeler de; *to call out,* appeler, (shout) crier; *to call to,* crier à.
camel, chameau, m.
can, pouvoir, savoir; *as soon as he could,* aussitôt que possible; *he could do it,* il pourrait le faire; *he can read,* il sait lire; *that cannot be,* cela ne se peut pas.
Canada, m.
Canadian, Canadien, du Canada.
canal, canal, m.
candle, (tallow) chandelle, f.; (wax) bougie, f.
canned provisions, conserves alimentaires, f. pl.
cannon-ball, boulet de canon, m.
canon, chanoine, m.
canonry, canonicat, m.
canvas, toile, f.
capable (of), capable (de).
Cape Breton, Cap-Breton, m.

capital, (finance) capital, m.; (town) capitale, f.
captain, capitaine.
capture, prendre; *to be captured,* se faire prendre.
card, carder.
cardinal, cardinal; *Cardinal R.,* le Cardinal R.
care, soin, m., garde, f., souci, m.; *to take care of,* avoir (prendre) soin de, prendre garde à; *to take care not to,* se garder de, prendre garde de; *take care!,* prenez garde!
care for, soigner, protéger.
career, carrière, f.
carefully, soigneusement, attentivement.
carpenter, charpentier, m.; *carpenter work,* charpenterie, f.
Carracci, Carrache.
carriage, voiture, f.; (railway) wagon, m.; *carriage door,* portière, f.
carriage-builder, carrossier, m.
carriage-building, carrosserie, f.
carry, porter; *to carry it against,* l'emporter sur; *to carry off,* emporter, enlever.
cart, charrette, f., chariot, m.
case, cas, m.; *in case of,* en cas de.
castigation, châtiment, m.
Castile, Castille, f.
castle, château, m.
cat, chat, m.
catch, attraper, prendre, surprendre, saisir; *caught in* or *by,* surpris de.
cathedral, cathédrale, f.
Catholic, catholique.
cattle, bétail, m. sing., bestiaux, m. pl.
cause, n., cause, f., raison, f., affaires, f. pl.
cause, v.a., causer; *to cause to lose,* faire perdre.
cease, cesser (de with infin.)
cede, céder.
celebrated, célèbre (par), fameux (par).
cellar, cave, f.

VOCABULARY.

centime, centime, m.
central, central.
centre, centre, m.
century, siècle, m.
cereals, céréales, f. pl.
certain, certain.
certainly, certainement, parfaitement, bien sûr.
certainty, certitude, f.
certificate, certificat, m.: *certificate of attendance*, c. d'assiduité.
chain, chaîne, f.
chair, chaise, f., (professor's) chaire, f.
chamber, chambre, f.
Champagne, (province) Champagne, f., (wine) champagne, m.
change, changer; *change color*, changer de couleur.
chapel, chapelle, f.
chaplain (to), aumônier (de), m., chapelain (de), m.
character, (nature) caractère, m., personnage, m., réputation, f.
charge, charge, f.
charming, charmant.
chase, chasse, f.
chastisement, châtiment, m.
cheer, animer, réjouir, égayer.
cheese, fromage, m.
chemical, chimique.
chemistry, chimie, f.
cherry, cerise, f.
cherry-tree, cerisier, m.
chestnut-tree, châtaignier, m.
chicken, poulet, m.
chief, adj., principal, le plus grand.
chief, n. chef.
child, enfant, m., or f.
chocolate, chocolat, m.
choose, choisir, élire, préférer.
Christendom, chrétienté, f.
Christian, chrétien: *the Most Christian King*, le Roi Très Chrétien.
Christianity, christianisme, m.

Christmas, Noël, m.; *on Christmas day*, le jour de Noël; (*Noël* is frequently fem. on account of the ellipsis of *fête*.)
church, église, f.
circumstance, circonstance, f.; *straitened circumstances*, gêne, f.; *under ordinary circumstances*, dans des circonstances ordinaires.
citizen, citoyen, bourgeois.
citizenship, rights of, droit de cité, m.
city, ville, f., grande ville.
claim, n., droit, m., titre, m.; *you have the first claim to*, vous avez droit le premier à.
claim, v. prétendre, demander, réclamer.
clasp, serrer, joindre.
class, classe, f.
clay, argile, f.
clear, adj., net.
clear, v.a., (land) défricher.
clearing, défrichement, m.
clearness, clarté, f.
clergy, clergé, m. sing.
clerk, commis.
clever, habile, adroit.
cleverly, habilement, adroitement.
climate, climat, m.
climb, monter, grimper.
cloak, manteau, m.
clock, (tower) horloge, f., (house) pendule, f.
close, fermer, clore, terminer.
closely, étroitement.
cloth, (general sense) étoffe, f. tissu, m., (wool or silk) drap, m.
clothing, habillement(s), m.
Clotilda, Clotilde.
clumsy, gauche, maladroit.
coach, (general sense) voiture, f., (cab) fiacre, m., (stage) diligence, f.
coachman, cocher, m.
coal, (general sense) charbon, m.; charbon de terre, m., 'houille, f.; *coals*, charbon.
coarse, rude, gros.
coast, côte, f., littoral, m.

coat, (general sense) habit, m.; *frock coat,* redingote, f.; *dress coat,* habit (noir), m.
cod, morue, f.; *cod-fishing,* pêche de la morue, f.
code, code, m.
coffee-house, café, m.
cold, froid.
collar, (horse) collier, m., (shirt) col, m., (coat) collet, m.
collection, collection, f., (poetry, etc.) recueil, m., (church) collecte, f., quête, f.
college, collège, m.
colonization, colonisation, f.
colonist, colon, m.
colony, colonie, f.
color, couleur, f.
colossal, colossal.
come, venir, arriver; *to come in,* entrer; *to come out,* sortir; *to come up,* survenir; *come and join,* venez joindre; *to come very near,* être tout près de, manquer peu de; *to come back,* revenir; *to come to see,* venir voir; *to come for,* venir trouver; *to come near,* approcher de; *to come down,* descendre; *to come running,* venir en courant.
comedian, comédien.
comedy, comédie, f.
comfort, bien-être, m., agrément, m., confort, m., commodité, f.
comfortable, confortable; *to make comfortable,* mettre à son aise, rendre confortable; *everything to make a family comfortable,* toutes les commodités que désirerait une famille.
comical, comique.
command, n., ordre, m., consigne, f., commandement, m.
command, v., commander, donner des ordres à; *to command him to do it,* lui commander de le faire.
commence, commencer (à with inf.)
commerce, commerce, m.
commercial traveller, commis voyageur, m.
commission, commissionner.

commit, commettre.
commodity, denrée, f.
common, commun, ordinaire; *to become common,* être une chose commune, arriver souvent.
commotion, commotion, f., émotion, f.
communicate, communiquer, (eccl.) communier.
compact, compact, serré.
companion, compagnon, m., compagne, f.
company, compagnie, f., société, f.; *keep company,* tenir compagnie (à); *in company with,* en compagnie de.
compare, comparer.
comparatively, comparativement, relativement.
comparison, comparaison, f.
compartment, compartiment, m.
compel, forcer, obliger; *I compel him to do it,* je le force à le faire; *I am compelled to do it,* je suis forcé de le faire.
competition, concours, m., concurrence, f.
complain, se plaindre (que with subj. or de ce que with indic).
complete, adj., complet, entier.
complete, v.a., achever.
completely, complètement, entièrement.
compliment, compliment, m.
comply, accéder, céder, acquiescer.
compose, composer, écrire; *to compose oneself,* se calmer.
composer, compositeur, m.
composition, composition, f.
compress, comprimer.
comprise, comprendre, contenir.
comrade, camarade, m. or f., compagnon, m.
conceal, cacher, celer.
conceited, suffisant.
conceive, concevoir, se figurer, s'imaginer; *to conceive to be used,* se figurer employé.
conception, conception, f., idée, f.

concerning, concernant, touchant, à l'égard de.
concierge, concierge, m. and f.
condemn, condamner.
condescend, daigner, condescendre.
condition, condition, f., circonstance, f.; *on condition that,* à condition que.
condole with, faire ses compliments de condoléance à.
condolence, condoléance, f.
conduct, conduire, diriger.
conducting, conducteur,-trice.
conductor, conducteur, m.
confer (on), conférer (à), accorder (à).
confess, avouer, confesser.
confine, enfermer, renfermer, limiter, borner.
conflict, conflit, m., lutte, f.
congratulate, féliciter, complimenter.
conifer, conifère, f.
connect, attacher, lier; *connected with,* ayant trait à, se rapportant à.
conquer, vaincre, conquérir.
conqueror, conquérant, m., vainqueur, m.
conscience, conscience, f.
consent, consentir.
consequently, par conséquent.
consider, considérer, regarder, reconnaître.
considerable, considérable, grand, important.
consist, consister (*à* with infin., *en* and *dans* with nouns.)
constrain, contraindre, comprimer.
construct, construire, bâtir.
construction, construction, f.
consul, consul, m.
consulting room, cabinet, m.
contain, contenir; *could not contain herself for joy,* ne se sentait plus de joie.
contemplation, contemplation, f.
contempt, mépris, m.

content, contenter; *to content himself with,* se contenter de.
contest, lutte, f.
continental, continental.
continue, continuer, poursuivre; *to continue on their way,* poursuivre (continuer) leur chemin.
contrary, on the, au contraire.
contrive, trouver moyen (de).
conundrum, énigme, f.
conventional, de convention.
conversation, conversation, f., entretien, m.
converse, parler, converser.
convert, convertir, transformer.
conviction, conviction, f.
convince, convaincre, persuader.
cool, frais, fraîche.
coolly, avec sang-froid.
cope with, tenir tête à.
copy, exemplaire, m.
cord, cordon, m., corde, f.
cork, (material) liège, m., (stopper) bouchon, m.
cork-oak, chêne-liège, m.
corn, Indian, maïs, m.; (In Lower Canada) blé d'Inde, m.
corner, coin, m., angle, m., extrémité, f.
corporal, caporal, m.
correct, corriger.
correctly, exactement.
correspondance, f.
Corsica, Corse, f.
cost, n., dépense, f., prix, m., frais, m.; *at my expense,* à mes dépens.
cost, v., coûter.
cottage, chaumière, f.
cotton, coton, m.
count, n., compte, m., (title) comte.
count, v., compter.
counter, comptoir, m.
countess, comtesse.
country, pays, m., campagne, f.; *in the country,* à la campagne.
countryman, (fellow-) compatriote; campagnard, paysan.

countrywoman, campagnarde, paysanne.
county, comté, m.
courage, courage, m.
course, cours. m. ; *of course*, bien entendu ; *in the course of time*, avec le temps.
court, n., cour, f. ; *at court*, à la cour.
court, v.a., faire la cour à, courtiser, rechercher.
courtier, courtisan, m.
cousin, cousin.
cover (with), couvrir (de), fermer ; *covered*, couvert, (carriage) fermée.
cow, vache, f.
cowardly, lâche, poltron.
crabbedly, d'une manière bourrue.
crane, grue, f.
create, créer.
creator, créateur, m.
crime, crime, m., forfait, m.
critic, critique, m.
criticism, critique, f.
crop, brouter, paître.
cross, n., croix, f.
cross, v.a., franchir, traverser.
crown, n., couronne, f., (coin) écu, m.
crown (with), couronner (de).
cruelty, cruauté, f.
crupper, croupière, f.
crusade, croisade, f.
crush, écraser, accabler.
crust, croûte, f.
cry, n., cri, m.
cry, v., crier, (weep) pleurer ; *to cry out*, s'écrier, crier fort.
cultivate, cultiver.
culture, culture, f.
cunning, rusé, fin.
cup, tasse, f.
cupboard, armoire, f., buffet, m.
cure, guérir.
curious, curieux.
cushion, coussin, m. ; *covered with cushions*, capitonné.

customer, pratique, client, f., m.
cut, n., coupure, f. ; page 54, use *coupé* p.p.
cut, cut off, v., couper, trancher, séparer ; *to cut off his head*, lui couper la tête ; *to cut up*, couper ; *to cut short*, abréger.

D.

Damietta, Damiette, f.
dance, danser.
danger, danger, m. ; *in danger of*, en danger de.
dangerous, dangereux.
dark, obscur, noir, de couleur foncée ; *after dark*, quand il fait nuit.
date, n., (fruit) datte, f., (time) date, f.
date, v., dater.
daughter, fille.
day, jour, m., journée, f. ; *all day (long)*, toute la journée ; *of our day*, de nos jours.
dead, mort, décédé.
deaf, sourd ; *to turn a deaf ear to*, faire la sourde oreille à.
deafness, surdité, f.
deal, a good, beaucoup (de).
dear, cher ; *dear me!*, mon Dieu !
death, mort, f. ; *on the death*, à la mort.
debt, dette, f. ; *for debt*, pour dettes.
deceased, décédé, défunt.
deceive, tromper.
December, décembre, m.
deciduous, à feuilles caduques.
declare, déclarer ; *to declare itself*, se déclarer.
deed, action, f., exploit, m.
deep, profond.
deeply, profondément, beaucoup.
defeat, n., défaite, f., déroute, f.
defeat, v.a., vaincre, défaire.
defence, défense, f.
defend, défendre.
defender, défenseur, m.
definitely, définitivement, d'une manière déterminée.

degree, degré, m., rang, m.
delicate, délicat.
delicious, délicieux.
delight, enchanter, plaire à, faire les délices de ; *delighted at,* enchanté de.
delightful, charmant, ravissant.
deliver, délivrer ; *to deliver up,* livrer.
demand, demander, réclamer.
democracy, démocratie, f.
depart, partir, sortir, s'en aller.
department, département, m.
deputy, député, m.
descend, descendre.
desert, n., désert, m.
desert, v., déserter.
deserve, mériter.
designation, désignation, f., nom, m.
desire, n., désir, m.
desire, v.a., désirer, vouloir, souhaiter.
despotic, despotique.
destroy, détruire, exterminer.
destructive, destructif.
detain, retenir.
determine, avoir l'idée de, déterminer (de with inf.), s'aviser (de).
deuce, diantre, m. ; *why the deuce?,* que diantre ?
development, développement, m.
devote, consacrer.
devour, dévorer.
dialogue, dialogue, m.
diamond, diamant, m.
dictate, dicter.
die (with), mourir (de).
difference, différence, f.
different, différent.
difficult, difficile, malaisé.
difficulty (in), difficulté (à), f. peine, f.
dig, creuser ; *to dig away,* creuser toujours, continuer à creuser.
dignity, dignité, f.
diminish, diminuer, amoindrir.

dine (off or upon), dîner (de).
dining-room, salle à manger, f.
dinner, dîner, m. ; *dinner-time,* heure de dîner, f.
direction, direction, f. ; *in the direction of,* dans la direction de, du côté de.
directly, immédiatement, tout de suite ; directement, étroitement.
disagreeable, désagréable, fâcheux.
discover, découvrir, trouver.
discoverer, celui qui découvrit, explorateur.
discovery, découverte, f.
discuss, discuter.
discussion, discussion, f.
disease, maladie, f., mal, m.
disgraceful, honteux, infâme.
dishonor, déshonneur, m., boue, f.
dislocate one's shoulder, se démettre l'épaule.
dismiss, congédier, renvoyer.
dismount, descendre.
display, make, faire parade (de), étaler.
displeased (with), mécontent (de).
displeasure, mécontentement, m., déplaisir, m.
disposal, disposition, f.
dispute, n., dispute, f., discussion, f.
disputed, en controverse.
disrespect, manque de respect, m., manque d'égards, m.
distance, distance, f., éloignement, m. ; *in the distance,* au loin.
distasteful, odieux, offensant.
distinction, distinction, f.
distinguish, distinguer ; *to distinguish oneself (for),* se distinguer (par).
distinguished (for), distingué (par).
distress, peine, f., détresse, f.
distressed (at), affligé (de).
distribution, distribution, f.
district, région, f., contrée, f.

disturb, troubler, déranger; *don't disturb yourself*, ne vous dérangez pas.
ditch, fossé, m.
divert himself, se divertir.
divide, diviser, partager.
divine, divin.
division, compartiment, m., division, f.
do, (as an auxiliary *do* is frequently omitted in translation. When *do* is used elliptically, the verb for which it stands is generally expressed in French); faire. (of health) se porter, aller; *to be done*, se faire; (finish) finir; *to have nothing to do with*, n'avoir rien de commun avec, n'avoir rien à faire avec; *as they always did*, comme ils faisaient toujours; *to do away with*), supprimer; *to do up hair*, coiffer; *to do without*, se passer de; *yes, I do*, oui.
doctor, médecin, docteur.
doctrine, doctrine, f.
dog, chien, m.
doge, doge.
Domenichino, le Dominiquin.
domestic, domestique, de famille.
domination, domination, f.
dominions, royaume, m., états, m. pl.
door, porte, f., (carriage) portière, f.
double, double, m.
doubt, n., doute, m.; *no doubt*, sans doute.
doubt, be doubtful, douter (de); *I doubt it*, j'en doute.
Dover, Straits of, Pas de Calais, m.
down, bas, en bas, à bas, (yonder) là-bas.
drama, drame, m.
dramatic, dramatique.
draw, tirer, attirer; *to draw out*, retirer; *to draw up*, rédiger, dresser; *to draw back*, retirer, tirer.
drawing-room, salon, m.
dread, crainte, f., effroi, m.
dreadful, affreux, terrible, épouvantable.

dreadfully, affreusement, terriblement.
drench, mouiller, tremper.
dress, v.a., habiller, vêtir; (wound) panser; *dressed*, habillé, mis, vêtu; *dressed in*, portant, habillé de, vêtu de.
drink, n., boisson, f.
drink, v.a., boire; *to drink to*, boire à la santé de.
drive, mener, conduire; aller en voiture, se promener; *to drive away*, chasser, conjurer; *to be out driving*, se promener; *to drive on*, partir, avancer; *to drive off*, partir; *to drive (nails)*, enfoncer; *to drive from*, chasser de.
drop, laisser tomber.
drown, v.a., noyer; *to drown, to be drowned*, se noyer.
drunken, ivre; *a drunken man*, un homme ivre, un ivrogne.
dry, adj., sec, aride.
dry, v.a., sécher, (wipe) essuyer; *to dry up*, dessécher.
dry-dock, bassin de construction, m., bassin de radoub, m.
duchess, duchesse, f.
duc, dû, duc.
duke, duc.
dull, lourd, assommant, (blunt) émoussé.
dunce, ignorant, âne.
during, pendant, durant.
duty, devoir, m.
dwelling, habitation, f., demeure, f.
dynamite, dynamite, f.
dynasty, dynastie, f.

E.

each, adj., chaque, tout; pron., chacun; *each other*, l'un l'autre.
eagerly, avec empressement, ardemment.
eagerness, empressement, m.
eagle, aigle, m.
ear, oreille, f.
earl, comte.
earliest, premier.

early, adj., précoce, premier, *at an early age*, quand il était encore jeune ; *at the early age of 20*, lorsqu'il n'avait que 20 ans.
early, adv., de bonne heure, tôt ; *earlier*, plus tôt, avant cela.
earnestly, ardemment.
earth, terre, f.
earthenware, faïence, f., poterie, f.
easily, facilement, aisément.
east, est, m., orient, m.
Easter, Pâques, m.s. ; *on Easter day*, le jour de Pâques.
eastern, oriental.
easy, facile, aisé.
eat, manger, dévorer.
Ebro, Èbre, m.
ecclesiastical, ecclésiastique.
echo, répéter.
economy, économie, f.
edict, édit, m.
edifice, édifice, m.
Edinburg, Édimbourg, m.
educate, instruire ; *he was educated*, il fit ses études.
education, éducation, f., instruction, f., enseignement, m.
educational, d'instruction, d'éducation.
effort, effort, m.
Egypt, Égypte, f.
eight, huit ; *eighth*, huitième, (kings, dates, etc.) huit.
eighteen, dix-huit ; *eighteenth*, dix-huitième, (kings, dates, etc.) dix-huit.
eighty, quatre-vingt(s).
either, ou, soit, l'un ou l'autre ; *either....or*, ou....ou ; *not...either*, ne pas....non plus ; *nor I either*, ni moi non plus.
Elba, Elbe, f., l'île d'Elbe, f.
Elbe, m.
elderly, d'un certain âge, entre deux âges.
elect, élire, nommer, choisir.
electricity, électricité, f.
elegant, élégant, distingué.

elevated, élevé, relevé.
eleven, onze ; *eleventh*, onzième, (kings, dates, etc.) onze.
elm, orme, m.
eloquence, éloquence, f.
else, autre ; *anything else*, n'importe quelle chose ; *every one else*, tout autre ; *nobody else*, personne (d') autre ; *nowhere else*, nulle part ailleurs.
elsewhere, ailleurs, autre part.
embark, s'embarquer (dans), (fig.) s'engager (dans).
emblem, emblème, m.
embrace, embrasser.
embroider, broder.
eminent, éminent.
emperor, empereur.
empire, empire, m.
employ, employer, se servir de, engager.
employed (in), occupé (à).
empress, impératrice.
empty, vider.
enable, mettre à même de, rendre capable de, mettre en état de.
enclose, renfermer, fermer, entourer.
encourage, encourager (à with infin.)
end, n., bout, m., fin, f., but, m. ; *to be at an end*, être fini ; *with that end in view*, dans ce but.
end, v., finir, terminer.
endeavor, tâcher (de with infin.)
endow (with), douer (de).
endure, supporter, endurer, souffrir.
enemy, ennemi, m.
energy, énergie, f., force, f.
engage in war, entreprendre la guerre.
engaged in, occupé à.
engine, machine, f. ; *steam-engine*, machine à vapeur.
England, Angleterre, f.
English, Englishman, anglais.
English Canadian, Anglo-Canadien.

English Channel, Manche, f.
engrave, graver.
engraver, graveur, m.
engraving, gravure, f.
enjoy, jouir (de), goûter.
enliven, animer, égayer.
enormous, énorme, très grand.
enough (to), assez (pour); *well enough,* assez bien; *more than enough,* plus que suffisant.
enter, v.n., entrer; v.a., entrer dans.
enterprise, entreprise, f.
entirely, entièrement.
entitled, be, avoir (le) droit à.
entrance, entrée, f.
entresol, m.
entrust, confier.
envy, n., envie, f.
envy, v., envier, porter envie à.
epic, épique.
epigrammatic, épigrammatique.
equilibrium, équilibre, m.; *to keep one's equilibrium,* garder l'équilibre.
equip, équiper, fournir, pourvoir.
era, ère, f.
erect, construire, élever, bâtir.
escape, échapper à.
especially, surtout, spécialement, particulièrement.
essay, n., essai, m.
essay, v., essayer.
establish, établir; *to establish oneself,* s'établir.
establishment, établissement, m., (firm) maison, f.
esteem, n., estime, f., respect, m.
esteem, v.a., estimer; *esteemed by,* estimé de.
Europe, f.
European, européen.
even, adv., même.
evening, soir, m., soirée, f.
event, événement, m.; *at all events,* dans tous les cas.
ever, jamais; *for ever,* à jamais, pour jamais; *hardly ever,* presque jamais.
evergreen, à feuilles persistantes, toujours vert.
every, chaque, tout, tous les.
everybody, tout le monde.
everything, tout, toute chose.
everywhere, partout.
evident, évident.
evidently, évidemment.
evil, mal, m.
exact, exact.
examination, examen, m., épreuve, f.
examine, examiner, interroger.
example, exemple, m., échantillon, m.; *for example,* par exemple.
exceed, dépasser.
excel, exceller, surpasser, l'emporter sur.
excellent, excellent, parfait.
except, sauf, excepté, à l'exception de.
exclaim, s'écrier.
excuse, excuser.
exercise, exercer.
exhausted (by), épuisé (de).
exile, (pers.) exilé, m., (banishment) exil, m.
exist, exister.
expansion, expansion, f.
expect, espérer, attendre, compter (sur).
expedient, expédient.
expedition, expédition, f.
expel, expulser, chasser.
expense, dépense, f., dépens, m. pl.; *at the expense of,* aux dépens de.
experience, expérience, f.
expert (in), habile (à).
explain, expliquer.
exploit, exploit, m.
explore, explorer, examiner.
export, exportation, f.
expose, exposer.
express, exprimer; faire témoigner.
expression, expression, f.

extend, v.a., étendre; v.n., s'étendre.
extensive, vaste, grand.
extent, étendue f., degré, m., point, m. : *to a certain extent*, jusqu'à un certain point.
extra, en sus, de plus.
extraordinary, extraordinaire.
extreme, extrême, grand.
extremely, extrêmement, fort.
extremity, extrémité, f.
eye, œil, yeux, m.

F.

fable, fable, f.
fabulist, fabuliste, m.
face, visage, m., figure, f.
facilitate, faciliter.
fact, fait, m.
fail, manquer, faillir, échouer ; (in business) faire faillite.
faint, faible, léger.
fairy, fée, f. ; *fairy tale*, conte de fées, m.
faith, foi, f.
faithful, fidèle.
fall, n., chute, f.
fall, v., tomber ; *to fall asleep*, s'endormir ; *to fall in*, tomber dedans ; *to fall back again*, retomber à sa place.
false step, faux pas, m.
fame, renommée, f.
familiar, familier.
family, famille, f.
famous (for), célèbre par, fameux par).
fancy, s'imaginer, se figurer ; *to fancy one's self to be ill*, s'imaginer malade.
far, loin ; *as far as*, aussi loin que, jusqu'à.
fare, prix des places, m., place, f.
farm, n., ferme, f. ; adj., agricole.
farmer, fermier, cultivateur.
farther, plus loin.
fascinating, charmant, attachant.

fashionable, à la mode.
fast, vite.
fasten, attacher.
fate, sort, m., destin, m.
fated, be, devoir.
father, père.
fatigue, fatigue, f.
fault, faute, f., défaut, m. ; *to find fault with*, trouver à redire à, critiquer, blâmer.
favor, faveur, f., grâce, f. ; *in favor of*, en faveur de ; *to do me the favor to*, me faire le plaisir de.
favorable, favorable.
favorite, favori,-ite ; *to be such a favorite with*, être tellement aimé de.
fear, n., crainte, f., peur, f.
fear, v.a., craindre, avoir peur de.
feast, se régaler.
feat, fait, m., chose, f., exploit, m.
feather, plume, f. ; *feather bed*, lit de plume, m.
February, février, m.
fee, honoraire, m.
feeble, faible.
feed, v.a., donner à manger à, nourrir ; v.n., paître ; *to feed upon*, se nourrir de.
feel, sentir ; *to feel himself*, se sentir ; *to feel sympathy in*, prendre part à ; *to be felt*, se faire sentir ; *to feel better*, se sentir mieux.
feeling, sentiment, m.
feigned, feint.
felloe, jante, f.
fellow, compagnon, m., camarade, m., garçon, m., enfant, m. ; (the word *fellow* is often omitted in translation) ; *thoughtless fellow*, étourdi ; *drunken fellow*, ivrogne ; *the poor fellow*, le pauvre garçon.
female, de femme.
fertile, fertile.
fetch, apporter, amener ; *to go (run and fetch*, aller (courir) chercher.
few, peu (de) ; *a few*, (adj.) quelques ; *fewer*, moins (de) ; *a few* (pron.), quelques-uns.
fierce, féroce, cruel.

VOCABULARY.

fifteen, quinze; *fifteenth,* quinzième, (kings, dates, etc.) quinze.

fifty, cinquante.

fig, figue, f.

fighting, combat, m., conflit, m.

figure, figure, f.

fill, remplir, occuper, tenir; *filled,* rempli, comble, complet.

finally, finalement, à la fin, enfin.

financial, financier.

find, trouver; *to find out,* découvrir, savoir; *the finest things to be found,* les plus belles choses qu'on puisse trouver.

fine, beau, bon, fin; *fine arts,* beaux-arts.

fine, in, enfin.

fine-looking, beau.

finger, doigt, m.; *first finger,* index, m.

finish, finir, terminer, achever; *to finish singing,* finir de chanter.

fire, n., feu, m.

fire at, v., tirer sur.

firebrand, tison ardent, m.

firewood, bois de chauffage, m.

first, premier;—*to die first,* mourir le premier; *first, at first,* d'abord, la première fois, en premier lieu.

fit, n., accès, m.

fit, adj., propre, convenable, à propos; *as one fit to,* comme quelqu'un propre à.

fit, v., aller (à), s'adapter (à), ajuster.

five, cinq; *fifth,* cinquième, (kings, dates, etc.) cinq.

flame, flamme, f., feu, m.

flattering, flatteur.

flax, lin, m.

flay, écorcher; *flayed alive,* écorché vif.

flee, s'enfuir, s'envoler.

fleet, flotte, f.

flesh, chair, f.

flight, take, prendre la fuite.

flock, troupeau, m.; (of a clergyman) ouailles, f. pl.

floor, plancher, m., pavé, m., fond, m., (story) étage, m.; *on the first floor,* au premier.

flow, couler; *flow through,* traverser.

fly, n. mouche, f.

fly, v.n. voler; *to fly away,* s'envoler; *to fly at,* s'élancer sur; *to fly down,* descendre; *to fly up,* voler (en haut), monter.

fob, gousset, m.

foliage, feuillage, m.

folks, personnes, f. pl., gens, pl.

follow, suivre; *as follows,* comme (il) suit, comme voici; *followed by,* suivi de.

following, suivant.

fond of, be, aimer (à).

food, nourriture, f.

fool, fou, bête, sot, imbécile.

foolish, bête, sot, simple.

foot, pied, m., bas, m.; *on foot,* à pied; *at the foot of,* au bas de.

footman, laquais, m., valet de pied, m.

foot-pavement, trottoir, m.

for, prep., pour, de, à cause de, pendant; (after *remercier*) de; *what he is there for,* pourquoi il y est; *for me to....,* pour que je....; *for ten days,* pendant dix jours; *what that is for,* à quoi ça sert.

for, conj., car, parce que.

forbid, défendre.

force, n., force, f.

force, v.a., forcer; *he forces him to do it,* il le force à le faire; *he is forced to do it,* il est forcé de le faire; *to force itself upon,* s'imposer.

foreign, étranger.

foreigner, étranger.

forest, forêt, f.

forestry, sylviculture, f.; *school of forestry,* école forestière.

fore wheel, roue de devant, f.; *fore wheels,* train de devant, m.

forget, oublier.

forgive, pardonner; *I forgive him for having offended me,* je lui pardonne de m'avoir offensé.

form, n., forme, f.

form, v.a., former, faire, façonner.

former, premier, celui-là.
fort, fort, m., forteresse, f.
fortified, fortifié.
fortnight, quinze jours.
fortunate, heureux.
fortunately, heureusement.
fortune, fortune, f.; *good fortune,* la bonne fortune, bonheur, m.
forty, quarante.
forward, en avant.
found, fonder.
founder, fondateur, m.
fountain, fontaine, f.
four, quatre; *fourth,* quatrième; (kings, dates, etc.) quatre; *four-wheeled,* à quatre roues.
fourteen, quatorze; *fourteenth,* quatorzième, (dates, kings, etc.) quatorze.
fox, renard, m.
frame, cadre, m.
franc, franc, m.
France, f.
Francis, François, Francis.
frankness, franchise, f.
Franks, Francs, m.pl.
Frederick, Frédéric.
free, adj., libre; sans rien payer.
free, v.a., libérer, délivrer.
French, Frenchman, français.
French Canadian, Franco-Canadien.
frequently, fréquemment, souvent.
friend, ami, m., amie, f.
frighten, faire peur à.
from, de, depuis, dès; *from that time on,* dès ce moment; *from me,* de ma part; *from....to,* de, depuis ....à, jusqu'à.
front, n., devant, m.; *in front of,* devant.
front on, v., donner sur.
fruit, fruit, m.
fruit-tree, arbre fruitier.
fry, v.n., frire; v.a., faire frire.
full, plein, tout, (carriage) complet.
full-grown, grand.

fun, plaisanterie, f.; *to make fun of,* plaisanter, se moquer de.
funeral, enterrement, m., funérailles, f. pl.
fur trade, pelleterie, f.
furious, furieux.
furnish, fournir.
furniture, meubles, m. pl.
future, avenir, m.; *for the future,* à l'avenir.

G.

gain, gagner, emporter; *to gain a victory,* remporter une victoire.
gallery, galerie, f.
Gallo-Romans, Gallo-Romains, m. pl.
garden, jardin, m.
garland, couronne, f., guirlande, f.
Garonne, f.
gas, gaz, m.
gather, v.a., cueillir, ramasser, assembler; v.n., se rassembler, se réunir.
general, n. général, m.; *in general,* en général.
generally, en général, généralement, ordinairement.
generation, génération, f.
generous, généreux.
Geneva, Genève, f.
genius, génie, m.
gentleman, monsieur, messieurs; (noble) gentilhomme, gentilshommes.
genuine, vrai, véritable.
German, allemand.
Germany, Allemagne, f.
get, gagner, obtenir, procurer, aller chercher, faire. *I haven't got it,* je ne l'ai pas; *to get on (well),* aller (bien); *to get in (on),* to get out (of carriage),* monter (dans), descendre; *to get to (into),* arriver à, atteindre; *to get there,* y arriver; *to get it put on,* le faire mettre; *to get off with,* en être quitte pour; *to get the better of,* avoir raison de; *to get home,* rentrer chez soi, arriver chez soi.
gift, don, m.

gigantic, gigantesque, très grand.
girl, fille.
girth, ventrière, f.
give, donner; (lectures) faire; *to give out*, succomber; *to be much given to*, avoir beaucoup d'inclination à, être très porté à; *to give up*, rendre, céder.
glad, content (de), enchanté (de).
gladly, volontiers.
glass, verre, m.; *glass door*, porte vitrée.
glassware, verrerie, f.
globe, globe, m.
glorify, glorifier.
glorious, glorieux.
glory, gloire, f., honneur, m.
glowworm, ver luisant, m.
go, aller, marcher, se rendre; (become) devenir; *to go into*, entrer dans; *to go away*, s'en aller, partir; *to go and carry*, aller porter; *to go for*, aller chercher, aller trouver; *to go along*, passer (dans); *as they went along*, chemin faisant; *how goes it?*, comment ça va?; *to go out*, sortir, se promener; *to go about it*, s'y mettre; *to go on*, se passer, avancer; *to go to see*, aller voir; *to make go*, faire marcher; *to go off*, descendre; *to go round*, faire le tour de; *to go to* (person), aller trouver, aller chez; *to go up*, monter; *to go down*, descendre; *to go in*, entrer; *to go without*, se passer de; *to go up to*, s'approcher de, approcher de; *to go by steam*, aller, marcher à la vapeur.
goat, chèvre, f.
God, Dieu.
godmother, marraine.
gold, or, m.
goldsmith, orfèvre, m.; *goldsmith's work*, orfèvrerie, f.
gone, be, être parti, n'y être plus.
good, adj., bon, brave; *to do good (to)*, faire du bien (à); *good gracious!*, mon Dieu!
good, n., bien, m.
good cheer, bonne chère.
good-humored, bon, enjoué.
good-natured, bon, d'un bon naturel.
gospel, évangile, m.
govern, gouverner, régir.
governor, gouverneur, m.
government, gouvernement, m., administration, f.
grace, grâce, f.; *your grace*, (archbishop, etc.) votre Grandeur, (duke) monsieur le duc.
graceful, gracieux, agréable.
graft, greffer.
grain, grain, m., (collective) grains, m. pl.
Grand-Duchy, Grand-Duché, m.
grandson, petit-fils.
grant, n., concession, f.
grant, v.a., donner, accorder.
grape, raisin, m.
grass, herbe, f.
grave, tombe, f., tombeau, m.
graze, brouter, paître.
great, grand, vaste, beaucoup de.
greatly, beaucoup.
greedy, gourmand; *greedy boy*, petit gourmand.
Greek, grec, grecque.
grindstone, meule, f.
grotesque, grotesque.
ground, terre, f., terrain, m.; *on the ground*, à terre; *to the ground*, à terre; *under ground*, sous terre.
ground-floor, (on the), rez-de-chaussée (au).
group, groupe, m.
grow, v.n., croître, pousser; *to grow weary*, s'ennuyer; v.a., produire, cultiver.
gruffly, rudement, d'un ton bourru.
grunt, grogner.
grunting, grognement, m.
guardian, gardien.
guards, gardes, m. pl.
guess, deviner.
guest, hôte, convive, convié.
guide, n., guide, m.
guide, v., guider.
guillotine, guillotine, f.

guilty, coupable.
guinea, guinée, f.
gulf, golfe, m.

H.

habit, habitude, f.
h a b i t a t i o n, habitation, f., demeure, f.
half, adj., demi ; *and a half*, et demi (e) ; *half-past*, et demi (e) ; adv., à demi, à moitié ; n., moitié, f.
hall, (public) salle, f., (entrance) vestibule, m.
halloo, crier.
hames, attelles, f. pl.
hammer, marteau, m. ; *Charles the Hammer*, Charles Martel.
hand, main, f. ; *on the other hand*, au contraire.
h a n d - r a i l, main coulante, f., rampe, f.
handsome, beau, élégant, gracieux, bien.
hang, pendre ; *to hang with garlands*, orner de couronnes.
happen, arriver, venir à ; *I happened to see him*, je l'ai vu par hasard : *if you happen to have*, si par hasard vous avez, s'il vous arrive à avoir.
happiness, bonheur, m.
happy, heureux.
harass, harasser.
harbor, port, m.
hard, adv., fort ; *harder*, plus fort.
hard, adj., difficile ; *to be hard at work at*, travailler ferme à ; (wood) dur.
hardly, à peine, c'est à peine si ; *hardly ever*, presque jamais.
hardy, robuste.
harm, mal, m. ; *to do him harm*, lui faire mal.
harness, n., 'harnais, m.
harness, v., 'harnacher.
harrow, 'herse, f.
hasten, se hâter (de).
hat, chapeau, m.

hate, 'haïr.
hatred, 'haine, f.
haughtiness, 'hauteur, f.
haughty, 'hautain, fier, altier.
have, (the compound tense is to be translated by the simple present with such phrases as *il y a* and *depuis*), avoir, falloir, devoir, faire : *to have brought*, faire apporter ; *to have to*, falloir, être forcé de, être obligé de ; *he has to do it*, il faut qu'il le fasse, il doit le faire.
hawthorn, aubépine, f.
hay, foin, m.
he, il, lui, celui ; *he himself*, lui-même.
head, tête, f., chef, m. ; *head first*, la tête la première ; *head of the bed*, chevet, m.
heading, for a, en tête.
head-quarters, rendez-vous, m.
health, santé, f.
hear, entendre, écouter ; *to hear of*, entendre parler de ; *you hear the bolt drawn back*, on entend tirer le verrou.
heartily, de bon cœur.
heat, n., chaleur, f.
heat, v.a., chauffer ; *to heat red-hot*, chauffer au rouge.
Heaven, ciel, cieux, m. ; *thank Heaven*, Dieu merci ; *good heavens!*, juste ciel!, grand Dieu !
heavily, lourdement, fort.
heavy, lourd.
hee haw!, hi han !
heed, pay, écouter, faire attention (à), prendre garde (de).
height, élévation, f., 'hauteur, f.
heir (to), héritier (de).
H e l e n a, Hélène ; *St. Helena*, Sainte-Hélène.
help, n., aide, f.
help, v., aider (à with inf.) ; *how can I help it?*, que voulez-vous que j'y fasse ?
hemlock, pruche, f.
hen, poule, f.
hence, c'est pourquoi, ainsi, aussi ; *hence it is that*, c'est pourquoi.

Henrietta, Henriette.
Henry, Henri.
her, adj., son, sa, ses; pron., la, lui, elle, celle.
herd, troupeau, m.
here, ici, là, que voici; *here and there,* çà et là; *here is (are),* voici; *here is one of them,* en voici un; *here!,* tiens!, tenez!
heretic, hérétique, m. or f.
hero, 'héros, m.
heroic, héroïque.
heroism, héroïsme, m.
hers, le sien, etc.
herself, se, elle, elle-même.
hesitate, hésiter.
hesitation, hésitation, f.
hidden, caché, intime.
hide (from), cacher (à).
high, 'haut, élevé, (of time) grand; *high and low,* du haut en bas.
highly, 'hautement, fort, beaucoup; jusqu'à un haut point.
Highness, Altesse, f.
hill, colline, f., côte, f., coteau, m.
him, le, lui; *himself,* se, lui, lui-même.
hinder, empêcher.
hind wheel, roue de derrière, f.; *hind wheels,* train de derrière, m.
hire, louer.
his, adj., son, sa, ses; pron., le sien, etc.; *an uncle of his,* un de ses oncles.
historiographer, historiographe, m.
history, histoire, f.
hitherto, jusqu'ici, jusqu'à présent.
hold, tenir, contenir, avoir, occuper; *it will hold them,* ils y tiendront; *to hold in veneration,* vénérer.
hole, trou, m.
holiday, fête, f., congé, m.; *national holiday,* fête nationale.
holy, saint.
home, chez soi, chez lui, etc.; *to return home,* rentrer chez soi, rentrer dans son pays; (industries, etc.) foyer, m.

homely, laid.
honestly, loyalement, franchement.
honey, miel, m.
honor, honneur, m.; *to do him the honor,* lui faire l'honneur.
hood, chaperon, m.
hoof, sabot, m.
hope, n., espérance, f.
hope, v.a., espérer, compter.
horn, corne, f.
horrible, horrible, affreux.
horror, horreur, f.; *to have a horror of,* avoir horreur de.
horse, cheval, m.
horse-chestnut, marronnier d'Inde, m.
horseman, cavalier, m.
horse-shoe, fer de cheval, m.
hospital, hôpital, m.
hospitality, hospitalité, f.
host, hôte, m.
hot, chaud.
hour, heure, f.
house, maison, f.; *at the house of,* chez; *my house, at my house,* chez moi.
how, comme, combien, comment, de quelle manière; (in sense of *what*) quel; *how little,* combien peu (de); *how many, how much,* combien; *how old are you?,* quel âge as tu?; *how many there are,* combien il y en a.
however, cependant; *however little it may be,* quelque petit qu'il soit.
hub, moyeu, m.
Huguenot, Huguenot, -e.
human, humain.
humane, bon, humain.
humanity, humanité, f.
humble, adj., humble.
humble, v., humilier.
hundred, cent; *sixteen hundred and twenty,* seize cent vingt, mil six cent vingt.
hunger, faim, f.

hungry, affamé ; *to be hungry*, avoir faim ; *to be getting hungry*, commencer à avoir faim.
hunt, n., chasse, f.
hunt, v., chasser, aller à la chasse (de).
hunting, chasse, f. ; *hunting-horse*, cheval de chasse, m.
hurry, be in a, se presser, se dépêcher, être pressé.
hurt himself, se faire mal.
husband, mari, époux.
hypocrite, hypocrite, m. and f.

I.

I, je, moi.
ice, glace, f. ; *ice-cold*, glacé, bien froid.
idea, idée, f.
idiot, idiot, imbécile.
idleness, paresse, f., fainéantise, f.
if, si.
ignorant, ignorant ; *to be ignorant of*, ignorer.
ill, adj., malade ; adv., mal.
ill-fated, malheureux.
ill-natured, bourru, rechigné, méchant (pour).
illness, maladie, f., indisposition, f.
imagine, s'imaginer, croire.
imitate, imiter.
immediately, immédiatement, tout de suite.
immortal, immortel.
impatience, impatience, f.
impatiently, impatiemment.
impériale, f.
impertinent, impertinent.
implement, outil, m.
imply, vouloir dire, signifier.
importance, importance, f.
important, important.
improvement, amélioration, f., perfectionnement, m.
in, dans, à, en, de ; y ; *in France*, en France ; *in Canada*, au Canada ; *in Paris*, à Paris ; *in Auvergne*, en Auvergne ; *in 1623*, en mil six cent vingt-trois ; (after superlative) de ; *in it*, y, dedans, là-dedans : *in a tone*, d'un ton ; *in the time of*, du temps de ; *in time*, avec le temps ; *in defending themselves*, à se défendre ; *in the middle*, au centre ; *in (inside)*, en dedans.
inclemency, intempéries, f. pl.
incognito, incognito.
indeed, en effet, en vérité ; vraiment !
independent, indépendant.
Indian, Indien, sauvage.
India-rubber, caoutchouc, m.
indicate, indiquer.
indication, indication, f.
industrious, laborieux, travailleur, diligent.
industry, industrie, f.
infallible, infaillible.
Infanta, Infante, f.
infirm, infirme, faible.
infirmity, infirmité, f.
inflict on, infliger à.
influence, influence, f.
information, information, f., renseignement, m.
inhabit, habiter.
inhabitant, habitant, m.
ink, encre, f.
inmate, habitant, pensionnaire.
inn, auberge, f.
inquire, demander, s'informer (de).
inquisitive, curieux, indiscret.
inscription, inscription, f.
insect, insecte, m.
inside, n., intérieur, m., dedans, m. ; adv., à l'intérieur, en dedans.
insignificant, insignifiant.
insist, insister.
insolently, insolemment.
inspiration, inspiration, f.
inspire, inspirer, dicter ; *to inspire him with courage*, lui inspirer le courage.
instance, for, par exemple.
instead of, au lieu de.
institution, institution, f.

instruct, instruire.
instruction, instruction, f.
instrument, instrument, m.
insult, n., insulte, f., injure, f.
insult, v., insulter.
insulting, outrageant, injurieux.
intend, avoir (l') intention (de), avoir dessein (de), vouloir; *to intend him for*, le destiner à; *intended*, destiné.
intent, appliqué, attentif.
intention, intention, f., dessein, m.
intently, fort attentivement.
interesting, intéressant.
interrupt, interrompre.
interruption, interruption, f.
into, dans, en; *into it*, y.
introduce, introduire, (of persons) présenter.
invitation, invitation, f.
invite, inviter.
inward, intérieur, intime.
Ireland, Irlande, f.
Irish, Irishman, Irlandais.
iron, n., fer, m.; adj., de fer.
island, île, f.
isle, île, f.
issue, sortir.
It, il, elle; le, la; ce, cela.
Italian, italien.
Italy, Italie, f.
itself, se, soi; lui-même, elle-même.

J.

Jack the Giant-Killer, Petit Poucet. (*Petit Poucet*, corresponds with *Tom Thumb* or *Hop o' my Thumb*, and *Jack the Giant-Killer*.)
Jansenist, janséniste.
January, janvier, m.
jealous, jaloux.
Jena, Iéna.
Jesuit, jésuite; *Jesuit college*, collège des jésuites, m.
jewel, joyau, m., bijou, m.
Jeweller, joaillier, bijoutier.
Jewelry, bijouterie, f.
Joan of Arc, Jeanne d'Arc.
join, joindre.
joiner, menuisier, m.
joiner work, menuiserie, f.
joint, jointure, f., joint, m.; *to put one's arm out of joint*, se démettre le bras.
joke, plaisanterie, f., tour, m., farce, f.
jokingly, en plaisantant.
jolting, cahotage, m.
journey, voyage, m., trajet, m.
joy, joie, f.
judge, juge, m., connaisseur, m.; *to be a good judge of*, se connaître en.
jug, pot, m.
July, juillet, m.
jump, sauter.
June, juin, m.
Jura Mountains, Montagnes du Jura, f. pl.
jurisprudence, jurisprudence, f.
just, adj., juste.
just, adv., juste, justement, un peu; *just as*, tout comme; *just turn*, tourne un peu; *just try*, veuillez tâcher; *just now*, tout à l'heure; *to have just been ill*, venir d'être malade.
justice, justice, f.
justly so, à bon titre.

K.

keep, tenir, garder, conserver; *to keep on*, continuer; *to keep quiet*, se taire; *to keep one's bed*, garder son lit; *to keep still*, rester tranquille; *to keep sheep*, garder les moutons; *to keep it from*, l'empêcher de.
key, clef, f.
kick, donner un coup de pied à.
kill, tuer, faire mourir.
kilometre, kilomètre, m.
kind, n., sorte, f.
kind (to), adj., bon (pour); *to be kind enough to*, avoir la bonté de, vouloir bien.

kindliness, bienveillance, f., bonté, f.
kindly, bienveillant, avec bonté; (with *remercier*) infiniment.
kindness, bonté, f., bienveillance, f.
king, roi.
kingdom, royaume, m.
kiss, embrasser, baiser.
kitchen, cuisine, f.
knee, genou, m.
knock, frapper; *to knock about*, traîner.
know, connaître, savoir; *to know how to*, savoir; *as is well known*, comme on sait bien; *I know this man*, je connais ce monsieur; *I know my lesson*, je sais ma leçon.
knowingly, finement.
known, connu; *much is not known*, on ne sait pas grand' chose.

L.

labor, labeur, m., travail, m.
Labrador, m.
lace, galon, m.; *all covered with lace*, tout galonné.
Lachine, f.
lack, n., manque, m.
lack, v., manquer (de).
lackey, laquais, m.
laconic, laconique.
lad, enfant, garçon.
ladder, échelle, f.
lady, dame; *my lady*, madame.
lake, lac, m.
lamb, agneau, m.
land, n., terre, f., terrain, m., pays, m.; *lands*, terres, propriétés, f. pl.
land, v., arriver, débarquer, aborder.
landing, palier, m., carré, m.
landlady, maîtresse d'auberge.
landlord, propriétaire, patron.
language, langue, f.
large, grand.

La Rochelle, f.; *from La Rochelle*, rochelois.
last, adj., dernier; *the last one*, le dernier; *at last*, à la fin, enfin, en dernier lieu.
last, v., durer.
lastly, en dernier lieu, enfin.
late, adv., tard, en retard; adj., dernier.
lately, dernièrement, depuis quelque temps.
later, adv., plus tard; adj., dernier.
Latin, latin, m.
latitude, latitude, f.
latter, dernier, celui-ci; *the latter*, celui-ci, ce dernier.
laugh, rire; *to laugh at*, rire de, se moquer de.
laughter, rire, m.
laureate, lauréat.
law, loi, f., droit, m.; *to study law*, étudier le droit, faire son droit; *law court*, cour de justice, f., tribunal, m.
lawn, pelouse, f.
Lawrence, Laurent.
lawyer, avocat, homme de loi, jurisconsulte.
lay, poser, mettre; *to lay down*, mettre, construire.
layer, couche, f., assise, f.
lazy, paresseux.
lead, conduire, mener.
leader, chef, m.
leaf, feuille, f., (door) battant, m.
league, lieue, f.
learn, apprendre; *to learn how*, apprendre à, apprendre la manière de.
learned, adj., savant.
learning, science, f.
least, adj., le moindre; adv., le moins.
leather, cuir, m.
leathern, de cuir.
leave, v.a., laisser, quitter; *to leave behind*, laisser (là); *leave it to me*, laissez-moi faire; v.n., partir (de).
leaven, levain, m.

VOCABULARY. 141

lecture, n., (course in college) cours, m., (each in the course) leçon, f., (public) conférence, f.; *he does not lecture to-day*, il ne fait pas son cours aujourd'hui.

lecture, v., faire un (des) cours, faire une conférence.

left, gauche.

leg, jambe, f.

legislature, législature, f.

leisure, at, à loisir.

lemon, citron, m.

lend, prêter.

length, longueur, f.; *at length*, à la fin.

lengthwise, en longueur.

less, adj., moindre; adv., moins.

lessen, diminuer, amoindrir.

lesson, leçon, f.

let, laisser; *let them take*, qu'on prenne; *to let you have them*, vous les laisser; *to let in*, laisser entrer, laisser passer.

letter, lettre, f.

level, niveau, m.; *on a level with*, de niveau avec.

liar, menteur.

liberty, liberté, f.

library, bibliothèque, f.

lie, n., mensonge, m.

lie, v.n., être couché; *lying*, couché, posé, placé; *lying on the ground*, (frequently merely) à terre; *to lie down*, se coucher.

lieutenant, lieutenant.

life, vie, f.; *in my life*, de ma vie.

lift (up), lever; *lift on to*, lever sur, mettre sur, charger sur.

light, adj., léger, (soil meuble); *lighter*, plus léger, moins lourd.

light, n., lumière, f., lueur, f.; *to come to light again*, se retrouver.

light, v.a., allumer.

lighten, éclairer, égayer.

like, comme, semblable (à), pareil (à); *like that*, comme cela; *and the like*, et de tels (fruits, etc.)

like, v.a., aimer, trouver (à son goût); *I like to do that*, j'aime à faire cela; *I should like to*, j'aimerais bien; *do you like it?*, l'aimez-vous?, est-ce à votre goût?; *to be much like*, ressembler beaucoup à.

Lille, f.

Limburg, Limbourg; *Limburg cheese*, fromage de Limbourg, m.

limit, n., bornes, f. pl.

limit, v.a., limiter.

limp, boiter.

linden tree, tilleul, m.

line, ligne, f.

linen, toile, f.; *linen cloth*, toile de lin, f.

linseed, graine de lin, f.

lion, lion, m.

lip, lèvre, f.

list, liste, f.

listen, écouter; *to listen to the numbers called out*, écouter l'appel des numéros.

lists, lice, f.

literary, littéraire; *literary man*, homme de lettres.

literature, littérature, f.

little, adj., petit; adv., peu; *a little*, un peu (de), quelque.

live, vivre, (dwell) demeurer; *still living*, encore en vie, qui vit encore; *to live upon*, vivre de.

liveried, en livrée.

living, n., vivre, m., vie, f.

locality, localité, f.

lodge, n., loge, f.

lodge, v., loger, se loger.

lodging, logis, m., logement, m.

lofty, haut, élevé, sublime.

Loire, f.

London, Londres, m.

lonely, solitaire.

long, adj., long; *to be a foot long*, être long d'un pied, avoir un pied de longueur, de long.

long, adv., longtemps; *not any longer, no longer*, ne.... plus; *long after*, longtemps après; *not to be long before*, ne pas tarder à; *so long as*, tant que; *before long*, avant longtemps.

look, n., regard ; air, m. ; *to take a look at,* voir à, regarder à, jeter un coup d'œil à.
look, v., regarder, chercher ; *to look at,* regarder ; *to look up,* chercher, lever les yeux (vers) ; *to look down upon,* regarder ; *to look like,* avoir l'air de ; *as he looks,* comme il en a l'air ; *to look askance at,* regarder de côté ; *to look for,* chercher.
loose, let, lâcher.
lord, seigneur, (as English title, untranslated) ; *the Lord's Prayer,* l'oraison dominicale, f., le Pater, m. ; *My Lord,* Monseigneur, Messeigneurs ; *the good Lord,* le bon Dieu.
lose, perdre ; *to lose oneself,* s'égarer.
loss, perte, f. ; *to be at a loss what to do with,* ne savoir que faire de.
loud, adj., 'haut, élevé ; adv., 'haut, fort.
Louvre, m.
love, n., amour, m.
love, v.a., aimer ; *loved by,* aimé de.
lover, (of things) amateur, m.
low, bas ; *in the Low Countries,* aux Pays-Bas.
lower, adj., inférieur.
lower, v.a., baisser.
Lower Canada, Bas-Canada, m. ; *in Lower Canada,* au Bas-Canada.
Lower Canadian, bas-canadien.
lowly, humble.
luckily, heureusement.
lucky, heureux.
luggage-rack, filet, m. (made of net-work in French carriages).
lumber, bois (de construction), m. ; *lumber shanty,* chantier, m. ; *lumber trade,* commerce de bois, m.
lunatic, lunatique, fou, aliéné.
Luxemburg, Luxembourg, m.
Lyons, Lyon, m.
lyric, lyrique.

M.

machine, machine, f.
machinery, machines, f. pl.
mad, fou.
madam, madame, Mme.
Madeleine, f.
maestro, maestro.
Magdalen Islands, îles Madeleine.
magistrate, magistrat.
magnanimous, magnanime.
magnificent, magnifique, superbe.
main, principal.
majesty, majesté, f.
majority, majorité, f.
make, faire, rendre ; *to make for,* prendre le chemin de, se diriger vers ; *to make oneself understood,* se faire comprendre ; *to make away with,* se défaire de ; *to make one's way,* se diriger ; *to make out (list),* faire, dresser ; *made up of,* composé de.
man, homme, valet ; *man of letters,* homme de lettres ; the word *man* is frequently omitted in translation ; *blind man,* aveugle ; *no man,* ne....personne.
manage, diriger ; *can you manage to?,* pourriez-vous par hasard ?
manifest, manifester, laisser voir.
manner, manière, f., façon, f. ; *in a manner,* d'une manière.
mantelpiece, cheminée, f.
manufacture, manufacture, f., industrie, f.
manufacturing, manufacturier.
many, beaucoup (de), bien (des) ; *a good many,* beaucoup ; *so many, tant (de) ; as many as,* jusqu'à, autant (de)...que ; *many a,* maint.
maple, érable, m. ; *maple sugar,* sucre d'érable, m.
march, n., marche, f., (month) mars, m.
march, v., marcher.
Margaret, Marguerite.
Maria, Marie.
mark, n., signe, m., marque, f.
mark, v., marquer, indiquer.
market, marché, m. ; *to market,* au marché.
marmalade, marmelade, f.

VOCABULARY. 143

marriage, mariage, m.
marry, épouser, (as father or priest) marier; *he gets married,* il se marie; *he is married,* il est marié.
Marseilles, Marseille, f.
marshal, maréchal, m.; *Marshal A.,* le Maréchal A.
martel, old form of marteau, hammer.
martyr, martyr, (fem.) martyre.
martyrdom, martyre, m.
master, maître.
masterpiece, chef-d'œuvre, m.
mat, natte, f.; (door) paillasson, m.
match, allumette, f.
material, matière, f., (building) matériaux, m. pl.
mathematics, mathématiques, f. pl.
matter, matière, f., affaire, f., sujet, m., chose, f.; *what is the matter?,* qu'y a-t-il ?, de quoi s'agit-il ?
maxim, maxime, f.
May, n., mai, m.; *in May,* au mois de mai.
may, v., pouvoir; *that may be,* cela se peut (bien); *it might have been,* il aurait pu être; *it might be,* il pourrait être; *you may have to wait,* il se peut qu'il faille attendre.
me, me, moi.
meadow, pré, m., prairie, f.
meaning, signification, f., sens, m.
means, fortune, f., moyen, m.; *by means of,* par le (au) moyen de.
meantime, en attendant, dans l'intervalle.
mediator, médiateur, m.
medicine, médecine, f.
meditate, méditer.
Mediterranean, Méditerranée, f.
meekly, humblement.
meet, v.a., rencontrer, (death) recevoir; v.n., se rencontrer; *to go to meet,* aller au-devant de, aller à la rencontre de.
meeting, rencontre, f.; *meeting place,* rendez-vous.
melody, mélodie, f.

member, membre, m.
memorable, mémorable.
memory, mémoire, f., souvenir, m.
menacing, menaçant.
mention, mentionner, parler de, nommer.
merchant, marchand, négociant.
merely, seulement, simplement.
message, message, m.
messenger, messager.
method, méthode, f.
Metz, Metz, f. (*t* silent).
middle, centre, m., milieu, m.; *the Middle Ages,* le moyen-âge.
midst, in the, au milieu.
mile, mille, m. (*kilomètre,* m., equal to five-eights of a mile, is the term most frequently used in France; while *lieue,* equal to three miles, is used in Lower Canada).
military, militaire.
milk, lait, m.
million, million, m.
mind, esprit, m.; *to call to mind,* se rappeler.
mine, le mien, etc.; *a friend of mine,* un de mes amis.
minister, ministre.
minority, minorité, f.
minute, minute, f., moment, m.
mischievous, méchant, (hurtful) nuisible.
miser, avare; *so great a miser,* si avare.
misfortune, malheur, m.
miss, v.a., manquer, remarquer l'absence de.
mission, mission, f.
missionary, missionnaire, m.
mistake, n., méprise, f., faute, f., erreur, f.; *by mistake,* par mégarde; *to make a mistake,* faire une faute, se tromper, commettre une erreur.
mistaken, be, se tromper.
mistress, maîtresse.
mockery, dérision, f.; *in mockery of,* se moquant de.
mode, mode, f., manière, f.

model, modèle. m.
moderate, modéré, modique.
modern, moderne.
modify, modifier, changer.
Mohammedan, Mahométan.
moment, moment. m. ; *at the moment when*, au moment où.
monarch, monarque, m.
monastery, monastère, m., couvent, m.
money, argent, m.
monotonous, monotone.
monster, monstre, m.
month, mois, m.
Montreal, Montréal, m.
Moors, Maures, m.pl.
moral, adj., moral.
moral, n., moralité, f., morale, f.
More, Sir Thomas, Thomas Morus.
more, plus (de), encore (des) ; davantage ; *much more*, beaucoup plus ; *no more, not any more*, ne...plus ; *no more do I*, ni moi non plus ; *two more*, encore deux ; *the more...the more*, plus...plus ; *more and more*, de plus en plus ; *more or less*, plus ou moins ; *will allow no more passengers to get on*, ne permettra plus de monter à qui que ce soit.
morning, matin, m., matinée, f. : *good morning*, bon jour ! ; *in the morning*, le matin.
morose, morose.
morsel, morceau, m.
Moscow, Moscou, m.
most, the, le plus, le mieux ; bien, très ; la plupart (de).
mother, n.. mère ; adj., maternel.
motto, devise, f.
mount, monter.
mountain, montagne, f.
mouse, souris, f.
mouth, bouche, f., (river embouchure, f.
mouthful, bouchée, f.
move, v.a., remuer, mouvoir, faire aller, transporter ; v.n., bouger, se remuer, (change residence) déménager.

Mr., Monsieur, M.
much, beaucoup, bien, très, fort ; *very much*, beaucoup, bien, très bien ; *so much*, tellement, tant (de) ; *too much*, trop (de) ; *as much as*, autant que.
mud, boue, f.
mulberry, mûre, f., (tree) mûrier, m.
murder, assassiner, tuer ; (language) écorcher.
museum, musée, m.
music, musique, f.
musical, de musique.
musician, musicien.
musket, fusil, m. ; *musket-bullet*, balle de fusil, f.
must, falloir, devoir ; *it must*, il faut (que) ; *you must have been*, vous avez dû être ; *I must...., je dois, il faut que je....
my, mon, ma, mes.
myself, me, moi, moi-même.

N.

nail, clou, m., (of finger or toe) ongle, m.
name, n., nom, m., appellation, f. ; *of the name of*, nommé ; *the name 'great,'* le nom de 'grand' ; *to mention his name*, le nommer ; *what's your name?*, comment vous nommez-(appelez-)vous ?
name, v., nommer.
namely, (à) savoir, c'est-à-dire ; on p. 87, may be omitted.
Nantes, m.
Napoleon, Napoléon.
nation, nation, f., peuple, m.
national, national.
native, natif,-ve, (of places) natal ; *native land*, pays natal, sol natal, patrie, f.
nature, nature, f.
natural, naturel.
naturally, naturellement, bien entendu.
navy, marine, f.

near, près (de); *to come near,* (s)approcher de, manquer de, faillir; *you came near being strangled,* vous avez failli (manqué d') être étranglé; *a village near by,* un village près de là; *the nearest....le....*voisin, le plus proche.

nearly, près de, à peu près, à peu de chose près, presque; *to be nearly,* manquer de.

necessary, nécessaire, indispensable; *it is necessary to,* Il faut; *it is not necessary to,* Il n'est pas nécessaire de.

neck, cou, m.; (of horse) encolure, f.; (of a bottle) col, m., goulot, m.; *to break one's neck,* se casser (se rompre) le cou.

need, n., besoin, m., nécessité, f., misère, f.; *I have need of,* j'ai besoin de, il me faut; *I shan't have any more need of them,* je n'en aurai plus besoin.

need, v., avoir besoin de; *I need....* il me faut...., il me manque....; *you need not come,* il n'est pas nécessaire de venir.

needless, inutile; *it is needless to say,* inutile de dire.

neglect, négliger (de before infin), manquer (à before infin.)

negligence, négligence, f.

negro, nègre.

neighbor, voisin: p. 104. *its neighbors,* les maisons voisines.

neighboring, voisin.

neither, ni, non plus; *neither....nor,* ni....ni (with *ne* before the verb).

never, jamais, ne....jamais.

new, (not old or worn) neuf, neuve; (different) nouveau, nouvelle; *quite new,* tout neuf; *New Year's day,* le jour de l'an.

New England, Nouvelle-Angleterre, f.

Newfoundland, Terre-Neuve, f., (takes no article).

New France, Nouvelle-France, f.

newly, nouvellement, récemment.

newspaper, journal, m., (*daily* = quotidien).

next, prochain, suivant; *next day,* le lendemain; *next morning,* le lendemain matin; *next week,* la semaine prochaine; *the next town,* la ville la plus proche, la ville voisine; *the next above,* celui au-dessus.

nice, bon, joli, fin; difficile; *nice taste,* bon goût.

night, nuit, f., soir, m., soirée, f.; *at night,* la nuit, le soir; *10 o'clock at night,* dix heures du soir; *12 o'clock at night,* minuit, m.; *late at night,* bien avant dans la nuit; *all night,* toute la nuit; *the other night,* l'autre soir.

night-fall, at, à la tombée de la nuit, à la nuit tombante, à la brune.

nightingale, rossignol, m.

nine, neuf; **ninth,** neuvième, (of kings, dates, etc.) neuf.

nineteen, dix-neuf; **nineteenth,** dix-neuvième.

ninety, quatre-vingt-dix.

no, adv., non, ne....pas; adj., nul, aucun, (ne)....pas un; *no one, nobody,* personne, nul; *no more,* pas plus, ne...plus; *no more do I,* moi non plus; *no less prudent than brave,* prudent autant que brave.

noble, nobleman, noble, gentilhomme.

noble, adj., noble.

noise, bruit, m., vacarme, m., tapage, m.

none, nul, aucun, pas un; personne; *he has lost none of his fire,* il n'a rien perdu de sa verve.

nor, ni, non plus; *neither...nor,* ni ....ni (with *ne* before verb); *nor is much known,* on ne sait pas beaucoup non plus; *nor do you,* (ni) vous non plus.

Normandy, Normandie, f.

north, nord, m.; adj., nord, septentrional, du nord; *in the north,* dans le (au) nord; *North Sea,* Mer du Nord, f.; *at....north latitude,* à (sous)....de latitude nord (septentrionale).

north-east, nord-est, m.; *north-eastern,* (du) nord-est.

north-west, nord-ouest, m.; adj., (du) nord-ouest; *at the north-west corner,* à la pointe nourd-ouest.

nose, nez, m., (of animals) museau, m.; *to speak through the nose*, parler du nez.

not, ne....pas, pas; *certainly not*, certainement non; *not one*, pas un (seul).

noted, distingué, fameux, célèbre; *noted for*, connu, célèbre, etc. par.

nothing, ne....rien, rien (when verb is unexpressed); *nothing certain*, rien de certain, de précis; *nothing but*, ne....rien que, ne.... que; *that's nothing to you*, cela ne vous regarde pas, ne (vous) fait rien; *there is nothing to laugh at*, il n'y a pas de quoi rire.

notice, n., avis, m.; *notice on pasteboard*, écriteau, m.

notice, v., remarquer, s'apercevoir de.

notion, notion, f., idée, f.; *to take the notion to*, s'aviser de.

novelty, nouveauté, f.

November, novembre, m.

now, maintenant, à present, (in exposition, argument, etc.) or; *just now*, tout à l'heure (past or future); *now and then*, de temps en temps, de temps à autre, par ci par là; *nowadays*, aujourd'hui, de nos jours.

nowhere, nulle part.

number, n., nombre, m., quantité, f.; (on doors and other objects) numéro, m.; *a number of*, plusieurs.

number, v., numéroter; (to be...in number) être au nombre de....

nurse, nourrir, allaiter; (the sick) soigner.

nut, noix, f.; (small) noisette, f.

O.

oak, chêne, m.
oath, serment, m.
oats, avoine, f. sing.
obey, v.n., obéir; v.a., obéir à.
object, objet, m., but, m.
objection, objection, f.; *I should have had no objection*, je n'(y) aurais pas fait d'objection, je ne m'y serais pas opposé.

obligation, obligation, f.; *to be under great obligations to*, avoir beaucoup d'obligations à.

oblige, obliger, (compel) obliger, forcer (à or de with infin.); *to be obliged to go*, être obligé (forcé) d'aller; *I am obliged to you*, je vous suis (bien) obligé.

obscure, obscur.

observation, observation, f.

observe, observer, remarquer; (to say to one that) faire observer à qn. que.

obstinacy, obstination, f.

obtain, obtenir, procurer, se faire délivrer.

occasion, n., occasion, f.; *on this occasion*, dans cette occasion.

occasion, v., donner lieu à, être (la) cause de.

occasionally, par occasion, parfois.

occupation, occupation, f.

occupy, occuper, remplir; *occupied in doing*, occupé à faire.

ocean, océan, m.

o'clock, not translated in French; *one o'clock*, une heure; *two o'clock*, deux heures.

octogenarian, octogénaire.

odor, odeur, f.

of, de; (made of) en, de; *an uncle of mine*, un de mes oncles, (famil.) un mien oncle; *how many are there of you?*, combien êtes-vous?

off, *I am off*, je m'en vais, me voilà parti; *to fall off his*..., tomber de son...; *to get off with*..., en être quitte pour....; *to dine off....*, manger à dîner, dîner de.

offend, offenser, blesser, froisser.

offer, offrir (de with infin), présenter.

office, office, m., service, m., (position) charge, f., emploi m., (place) bureau, m., cabinet, m., étude, f.

officer, officier, m.

often, souvent.

ogre, ogre, m.

oh! oh!

oil, huile, f.; (in Amer., *coal-oil*) pétrole, m.

old, vieux, vieille, ancien ; âgé ; *old man,* vieillard ; *how old are you?,* quel âge avez-vous ? *I am ten,* j'ai dix ans.

olive, olive, f.

olive-tree, olivier, m.

omnibus, omnibus, m.

on, sur, à, en, dans ; *on the luggage-rack,* dans le filet ; *to lift on (to) his horse,* charger sur son cheval ; *on the death of,* à la mort de ; *an attack on,* une attaque contre ; *on Tuesday,* (le) mardi ; *on the 10th,* le dix ; *on the morning of,* le matin de ; *on the evening when,* le soir où ; *on this side,* de ce côté ; *closed on 3 sides,* fermé sur 3 côtés ; *on it,* dessus, y ; *on board,* à bord de ; *on the first floor,* au premier (étage) ; *on receiving,* en recevant ; *on the east, etc.,* à l'est ; p. 82, *they are on,* ils portent sur ; *on one (this) occasion,* dans une (cette) occasion ; *on the second visit,* à la seconde visite ; *to get on,* avancer, faire des progrès, aller, marcher ; *how does he get on (with his studies)?,* quels progrès fait-il (dans ses études) ? ; *from that day on,* à partir de ce jour ; *so on,* ainsi de suite.

once, une fois, autrefois ; *once upon a time there was,* il y avait une fois ; *at once,* aussitôt, immédiatement, tout de suite, à l'instant ; *once more,* encore une fois.

one, un, une ; *the one who,* celui, celle qui ; *the last one,* le dernier ; *any one,* quelqu'un, n'importe qui ; *the heavy ones,* les lourds ; *no one,* personne, nul ; *not one,* pas un (seul) ; *said one,* dit l'un ; *in one of the houses,* dans (l') une des maisons ; *may be in one,* ne font qu'un ; *one M. N.,* un certain M. N. ; *as one fit to,* comme étant propre à.

one, pron., on.

one-horse, adj., à un cheval.

only, adj., seul, unique ; adv., ne.. ..seulement ; (beginning of clause) seulement ; *not only,* non seulement ; *you have only to say so,* vous n'avez qu'à le dire.

open, v.a., ouvrir ; v.n., s'ouvrir, ouvrir ; *to open on,* donner sur.

open(ed), adj., ouvert.

opera, opéra, m.

operation, opération, f. ; *by this operation,* sur cette opération.

opinion, opinion, f., jugement, m.

opportune, opportun, à propos.

opposite, opposé, en face (de) ; *on the opposite side,* de l'autre côté ; n., opposé, m., contraire, m.

or, ou.

orange, orange, f.

orator, orateur.

order, n., ordre, commandement, m. ; (on bank) mandat, m. ; (post-office) mandat-(de) poste ; *by the order of,* par (l')ordre de ; *to give orders that,* ordonner que, donner (l')ordre que (with subjunct.) ; *out of order,* dérangé, détraqué ; *in order to,* pour, afin de, dans le but de.

order, v., ordonner, dire ; *to order somebody to do something,* ordonner à qn. de faire qch. (on p. 49 use *dire*) ; *he was ordered by an officer to go,* un officier lui ordonna d'aller.

ordinary, ordinaire.

organize, organiser, établir.

origin, origine, f., source, f. ; *of lowly origin,* d'humble origine.

original, original, primitif, (sin) originel.

Orleans, Orléans, m. ; but note that *New Orleans* is La Nouvelle-Orléans, f.

ornamental, d'ornement, (of trees) d'agrément.

other, autre ; *others,* d'autres, *any other,* tout(e) autre, n'importe quel(le) autre ; *on the other hand,* d'autre part.

ought, devoir (pres. indic., or conditional) ; *you ought to come,* vous devriez venir ; *you ought to have come sooner,* vous auriez dû venir plus tôt, il fallait venir, etc.

out, hors (de), dehors, sorti ; (fire, light) éteint ; *out of breath,* hors d'haleine, essouflé ; *to give out on the way,* rester en route ; *take.... out of,* prendre....dans (see p. 67, note) ; *made (out) of wood,* fait en (de) bois ; *out of the window,* par la fenêtre ; *out in out driving, riding, walking,* is usually not translated.

outer, extérieur.
outlay, déboursé, m.
outlive, survivre à.
outside (of), prep., hors de, en dehors de; adv., dehors, au dehors, à l'extérieur; adj., du dehors, extérieur; *from the outside*, du dehors, de l'extérieur; *the outside* (of omnibus, diligence, etc.), impériale, f.
over, prep., sur, au-dessus (de), par-dessus, au delà de; adv., dessus, au-dessus, par-dessus, au delà; (finished) passé, fini, terminé; *to gain a victory over*, remporter une victoire sur; *triumph over*, triompher de; *to pass over*, passer sur, (above) par-dessus.
over-excite, surexciter.
overhear, entendre par hasard, surprendre; *overheard him*, surprit sa réflexion.
oversee, surveiller.
oversight, inadvertance, f., oubli, m.; (careless) négligence, f.
owing to, à cause de, grâce à.
own, adj., propre; *his, her own*..... son propre...; pron., *his, her own*, le sien, etc.; *of his own*, p. 48, pour lui-même, qui serait bien à lui.

P.

page, page, f.; (boy) page, m.
pailful, seau, m.
pain, n., douleur, f., mal, m.; peine, f.; *took every pains to*, se donnait bien de la peine (du mal), toutes les peines du monde, pour.
pain, v., faire mal à; (fig) faire de la peine à.
painfully, douloureusement.
paint, peindre.
painter, peintre.
painting, peinture, f., tableau, m.; (canvas) toile, f.
palace, palais, m.
Palestine, Palestine, f., Terre-Sainte.
palisade, palissade, f.
Pantheon, Panthéon, m.

pantry, garde-manger, m., office, m.
paper, papier, m.; (newspaper) journal, m.
parcel, paquet, m.
pardon, pardon, m., grâce, f.; *I ask (beg) your pardon (for)*, je vous demande pardon (de); *pardon me*, pardon.
pare, (fruit) peler, (one's nails, horse's hoof) rogner.
parents, parents.
Paris, m.; adj., de Paris, parisien.
parish, (ecclesiast.) paroisse, f.; *parish priest*, curé.
parishioner, paroissien.
park, parc, m.
parrot, perroquet, m., perruche, f.
parson, prêtre, ministre, pasteur.
part, (of whole) partie, f., (share) part, f., (of a country) région, f., (played) rôle, m.; *to form part and parcel of*, faire partie intégrante de; *in all parts of*, dans toutes les parties de, partout dans (en).
particularly, particulièrement, surtout.
party, (law and pleasure) partie, f., (milit. and faction) parti, m.; *to be one of a party*, être d'une partie.
pass, passer, (pass by....) passer devant, à côté de....; *3 young men passed by*, 3 jeunes gens passaient; *to pass that way*, passer par là; *to pass oneself off for*, se faire passer pour.
passage, traversée, f.; (in house) couloir, m.; (wider) corridor, m.
passenger, voyageur; (on boat only) passager.
passer-by, passant.
passion, (in general) passion, f.; (anger) colère, f.; *in a passion*, en colère; *in a violent passion*, dans une colère violente.
pasteboard, carton, m.; (see "notice.")
Pat, Patrick, Patrice.
pat, v., caresser (flatter) de la main.
patient, n. malade; (about to be executed or operated upon) patient.
patient, adj., patient, résigné.

VOCABULARY. 149

patriarch, patriarche.
patriotic, patriotique.
patron, patron, protecteur.
patronage, patronage, m., protection, f.
Paul, (in French short open o).
pay, payer; *to pay (a person), to pay for (a thing),* payer une personne, une chose; *to pay some one for something,* payer qch. à qn.; *to pay some one for doing something,* payer qn. pour faire qch.; *the compliments paid him,* les compliments qu'on lui faisait (fit); *to pay a visit,* faire une visite; *we pay for the best,* nous payons pour avoir le mieux.
pea, pois, m.
peace, paix, f., tranquillité, f., ordre, m.; *in peace,* en paix.
peaceful, paisible.
peacefully, paisiblement, tranquillement.
peach, pêche, f.
pear, poire, f.
pearl, perle, f.
pear-tree, poirier, m.
peasant, paysan; *peasant woman,* paysanne f.; adj., de paysan.
peculiar, particulier, singulier, bizarre.
peculiarity, particularité, f.
peer, pair, m.
pen, plume, f.
penetration, pénétration, f.
Peninsula, Péninsule, f.
people, peuple, m., nation, f.; gens, m. pl. (adj. preceding is generally fem.), personnes, f. pl., monde, m., habitants, m. pl.; on p. 25, *people said,* il y avait des personnes (des gens) qui disaient; (indefinitely) on; *a good many people,* beaucoup de gens, bien des personnes, (familiar) pas mal de gens (monde).
perfect, parfait, complet.
perhaps, peut-être.
Périgord, m.
peril, péril, m., danger, m.
period, période, f.

perish, périr.
permission, permission, f.; *to ask (give) permission to,* demander (donner) la permission de.
persecution, persécution, f.
person, personne, f.; *in person,* en personne.
personage, personnage, m.; personne, f.
persuade, persuader (de with infin.)
pertain to, se rattacher à, se rapporter à, avoir rapport à.
pestilence, peste, f.; *a pestilence,* la peste.
pet, favori, mignon; animal.
Peter, Pierre.
petition, pétition, f.; on p. 56, use the obsolete word *placet,* m.
petitioner, pétitionnaire.
Petræa, Pétrée, f.
phenomenon, phénomène, m.
philosopher, philosophe.
philosophy, philosophie, f.
phylloxera, phylloxéra, m.
physical, physique, de corps.
physician, médecin, docteur, (for *physicien,* see next line).
physicist, physicien.
physics, physique, f. sing.
Picardy, Picardie, f.
pick up, ramasser, soulever; p. 34, *as he picked up his wheelbarrow,* etc., qui soulève la brouette pleine de terre et la roule au loin, (or, simply and familiarly) et file avec.
picture, peinture, f., tableau, m.; (engraving) gravure, f., image, f.
piece, pièce, f., morceau, m.; *ten cent piece,* pièce de dix sous, (in France) de cinquante centimes.
pierce, percer, passer à travers de.
piety, piété, f.
pig, porc, m., cochon, m.
pill, pilule, f.
pillar, pilier, m., colonne, f.
pinch, n., (of snuff) prise.
pinch, v., pincer.
pine, pin, m.

pious, pieux, dévot, (the latter often disparagingly).
pit, fosse, f., trou, m.
pitcher, cruche, f.
pity, pitié. f.; *to have (take) pity on*, avoir (prendre) pitié de.
place, n., place, f., endroit, m., lieu, m., (seat) siège m., place, f.; *meeting place*. le (lieu du) rendez-vous; *to take place*, avoir lieu: *if I were in your place*, (si j'étais à votre place; *in the first place*, (tout) d'abord, pour commencer.
place, v., placer, mettre; p. 108, *placed*, attelé.
plain, uni, plat, simple; évident; *plain-looking*, laid.
plainly, simplement.
plan, plan, m., projet, m.
plant, n., plante, f.
plant, v., planter.
platform, plate-forme, f.
play, n., jeu, m., (drama) pièce, f.
play, v., jouer, représenter.
please, plaire (à), faire plaisir (à); contenter; *if you please*, s'il vous plait; *hard to please*, difficile, difficile à contenter.; *to be pleased with*. être content de; *I should be very much pleased*, je serais très content, cela me ferait beaucoup de plaisir; *your Majesty will please to observe*, votre Majesté voudra bien remarquer.
pleasure, plaisir, m.; *to take pleasure in*. prendre plaisir à.
plot, complot, m., trame, f.; (of play) intrigue, f., trame, f.
plough, n., charrue, f.
plough, v., labourer (la terre), sillonner (la mer, etc.)
pluck, (flower, fruit) cueillir.
plus, plus.
pocket, poche, f.; *he put it in his pocket*, il le mit dans sa poche.
pocket-book, portefeuille, m.
poem, poème, m., poésie, f.; *his poems*, ses poésies.
poet, poète, m.
poetic(al), poétique.
poetry, poésie, f.

point, n., (spot, place, dot, question) point, m.; (sharp point) pointe, f.; *in point of*, quant à, sous le rapport de, en fait de.
point, v., *to point at*, montrer du doigt; *to point to, to point out*, indiquer, montrer.
poison, n., poison, m.
poison, v., empoisonner, tuer.
pole, perche, f.; (of a carriage) timon, m.
policy, politique, f.
polish, polir; (floor) frotter; *polished*, (eloquence) raffinée, (satire) fine.
polite, poli, attentif.
politely, poliment.
political, politique; *political economy*, économie politique, f.
politics, politique, f. sing.
pompously, avec emphase.
poor, pauvre; *the poor*, les pauvres.
pope, pape, (le) saint-père.
poplar, peuplier, m.
population, population, f.
populous, peuplé.
port, port, m.
porter, (of door) portier, (now generally) concierge.
portion, portion, f., (share) part, f.: *in portions*, par portions.
portrait, portrait, m.; on p. 53, *to make portraits of*, peindre.
Port Royal, Port-Royal.
position, place, f., position, f., charge, f.
possess, posséder, avoir.
possession, possession, f.; *to take possession of*, prendre possession de, s'emparer de.
post, (letters) mettre (jeter) à la poste.
postage-stamp, timbre-poste, m., pl. timbres-poste.
posterity, postérité, f.
postscript, post-scriptum, m. (pronounce po-skri-ptom).
pot, marmite, f., pot, m.; *in the pot*, au pot.
potato, pomme de terre, f.

poultice, cataplasme, m.; *bread, linseed poultice,* cataplasme de mie de pain, de farine (de graine) de lin.
pour, verser, répandre.
power, pouvoir, m., force, f., puissance, f.; *divine power,* puissance divine.
practice, pratique, f., usage, m.
practise, pratiquer.
prairie, prairie, f., savane, f.
praise, louer, faire l'éloge de.
pray, prier; *pray* as elliptical for *I pray,* je vous (en) prie, (or often) s'il vous plaît.
prayer, prière, f., supplication f.; *Lord's Prayer,* oraison dominicale, f.; Pater, m.
preach, prêcher.
precede, précéder.
precious, précieux, cher.
precisely, précisément, justement, juste.
prefer, préférer (de with infin.), aimer mieux.
prejudice, préjugé, m., prévention, f.
prejudiced, prévenu.
prelate, prélat.
prepare, préparer.
prescription, (med.) ordonnance, f.
presence, présence, f.; *in presence of,* devant; *in his presence,* en sa présence, sous ses yeux.
present, adj., présent, (now existing) actuel; *at present,* à présent, actuellement; *to be present at,* assister à.
present, v.a., présenter.
presently, tout à l'heure, bientôt.
preserve, préserver, conserver.
presumption, présomption, f., assurance, f., audace, f.
pretext, prétexte, m.
pretty, adj., joli, gentil; (ironically) beau; adv., assez, passablement.
prevent, empêcher.
Preville, Préville.
prey, proie, f.

price, prix, m.; *moderate price,* prix modique.
pride, orgueil, m., fierté, f.
priest, prêtre, ecclésiastique; *parish priest,* curé.
prince, prince; *Prince Alfred,* le prince Alfred.
princess, princesse.
principal, principal, premier; *my principal business is,* pour moi la chose principale est.
principle, principe, m.
printing, impression, f.; (art) imprimerie, f.
prison, prison, f.; *in prison,* en prison.
prisoner, prisonnier; *to take one prisoner,* faire qn. prisonnier, prendre.
privilege, privilège, m.
privileged, privilégié.
prize, évaluer; *prize highly,* tenir beaucoup à, estimer beaucoup.
probable, probable.
probably, probablement.
probity, probité, f.; *of probity,* probe.
problem, problème, m.
proceed, aller, se rendre, continuer son voyage, pénétrer, pousser; *proceeded up the river,* continua à remonter le fleuve, remonta le fleuve.
proclaim, proclamer, promulguer.
proclamation, proclamation, f., promulgation, f.
produce, produire, faire naître; p. 76, voir naître; (to play) représenter, jouer.
product, produit, m.
production, production, f.; (of a play) représentation, f.
profess, professer, affirmer, prétendre; *professes to have sat,* prétend s'être toujours assis.
profession, profession, f., état, m.
professor, professeur.
proficient, versé, très fort (*in* = en).
profit, bénéfice, m.; *clear profit,* bénéfice net.

profound, profond.
progress, progrès, m.; (very frequently plur.) les progrès: *to make progress,* faire des progrès.
promise, promettre.
pronounce, prononcer; *to pronounce upon,* prononcer sur, juger de.
proper, propre, convenable; *the proper station,* la station voulue.
properly, comme il faut, convenablement; *shut it properly,* (re-)fermez-le bien; *properly speaking,* à proprement parler.
proportion, proportion, f.
proposition, proposition, f.
prospect, aspect, m., vue, f., point de vue, m., coup d'œil, m.
protect, protéger, garantir (*from* de)
protection, protection, f.
Protestant, protestant.
Protestantism, protestantisme, m.
proud (of), fier (de), orgueilleux.
prove, prouver, démontrer, établir.
provide, pourvoir, fournir; *provide oneself with,* se pourvoir de, se munir de; *to provide for,* pourvoir à; *provided with (springs),* muni de.
providence, providence, f.
province, province, f.; *in the Provinces,* en province; p. 86, *to a friend in the Provinces,* "à un Provincial de ses amis."
provincial, de province.
provisions, provisions, f. pl., vivres, m. pl., comestibles, m. pl.
prudent, prudent, sage.
Prussia, Prusse, f.
Prussian, prussien, de Prusse.
pshaw! bah!
pseudonym, pseudonyme, m.
public, public, -que; *public buildings,* monuments, m. pl.
publication, publication, f.
publish, publier, éditer, faire paraître; *just published,* vient de paraître; *was first published,* parut (fut publié) pour la première fois.

pull, tirer.
pulpit, chaire, f.
pumpkin, citrouille, f., potiron, m.
purchase, acheter, acquérir.
purpose, but, m., dessein, m.; *for the purpose of,* dans le but (le dessein, l'intention) de, à l'effet de; *on purpose to,* tout exprès pour, expressément pour.
pursue, poursuivre.
purveyor, fournisseur (*to*=de).
puss, minet, minette.
put, mettre, placer, poser; *to put in,* y mettre, mettre dedans (often simply mettre); *to put on,* mettre, (a horse-shoe again) remettre; *to put out (of joint),* démettre; *had put me in the drawing-room,* m'avait établi dans, etc.; *to put to, i.e. to put a horse into a carriage,* etc., atteler; *to put into the Bastille,* mettre (jeter) à la Bastille.
puzzle, intriguer, embarrasser.
Pyrenees, Pyrénées, f. pl.

Q.

quack, (quack-doctor) charlatan, empirique.
quadrangle, quadrilatère, m.
quality, qualité, f., excellence, f.
quantity, quantité, f.
quarrel, querelle, f., dispute, f.
quarter, n., (fraction) quart, m.; (three months) trimestre, m.; *a quarter of a...,* un quart de...
quarter, v.a., (troops) faire loger.
quay, quai, m.
Quebec, Québec, m.
queen, reine; *queen of Charles I.,* femme de Charles Ier..
quell, étouffer, réprimer.
question, n., question, f., demande, f.
question, v., questionner, interroger.
quick, vif; (reply) prompt; n. (flesh) vif, m., chair vive, f.; *that they should not get into the quick,* afin qu'ils ne le piquassent pas (jusqu' au vif, (or better) pour les empêcher de piquer (jusqu' au vif.

quickly, vite, rapidement, promptement, brusquement.
quiet, tranquille, calme : *a quiet place*, endroit retiré, lieu calme et hors du bruit ; *to keep quiet*, (se) tenir tranquille, se taire.
quietly, tranquillement, doucement.
quite, tout, tout à fait ; *quite as...*, tout aussi... ; *quite well*, très bien ; *quite a business*, toute une affaire.

R.

race, race, f., (contest) course, f. ; *to run a race with*, see under "run."
race-horse, cheval de course, m.
radical, radical.
railway, chemin de fer, m. ; *railway line*, ligne de chemin de fer, f.
rain, pluie, f.
raise, lever, élever, (a heavy weight, a person) soulever, (crop) cultiver ; *to raise again*, relever ; *to raise the siege*, lever le siège ; *to raise...against oneself*, s'attirer.
rake, râteau, m.
rank, rang, m. ; *elevated rank*, haut rang.
rapid, adj., rapide ; n. (in a river) rapide, m.
rapidly, rapidement, vite.
Raphael, Raphaël (Sanzio).
rare, rare.
rarely, rarement.
rascal, coquin, fripon, gredin.
rat, rat, m.
rather, plutôt ; (a little) assez, un peu.
reach, atteindre, (re)gagner, parvenir à, arriver à ; *to reach the top*, gagner le sommet ; *will reach...well enough*, arrivera bien à...
read, lire, parcourir ; *to read again*, relire.
reading, n. (act, subject-matter) lecture, f.
ready, prêt, prompt ; (on the table) servi ; *to get a horse ready*, préparer un cheval.

real, réel, véritable, vrai.
realise, réaliser.
really, réellement, en réalité, vraiment, en effet ; *I really don't know*, je n'en sais réellement rien ; *to find out who he really was*, pour savoir exactement qui il était.
rear, n., derrière ; adj., de derrière ; *rear block*, bâtiment sur cour, m.
reason, raison, f. ; *what is the reason*, quelle en est la raison.
rebellion, insurrection, f., révolte, f.
recall, rappeler.
receive, recevoir, accueillir.
receipt, (business) reçu, m., quittance, f. ; (recipe) recette, f.
recognise, reconnaître.
recollect, se souvenir de, se rappeler.
reconnoitre, reconnaître.
records, archives, f. pl.
record, v., enregistrer ; *recorded on the r.*, enregistré au c.
recover, v. a., recouvrer, retrouver ; *to recover one's breath*, reprendre haleine, v.n., se rétablir, se remettre, revenir ; *being recovered*, étant remis.
rectification, rectification, f., redressement, m.
red, rouge, (lips, mouth) vermeil ; (hair) roux ; *red-hot*, (chauffé au) rouge, (coals) ardent.
Red Riding Hood, Little, Le petit Chaperon rouge, m.
refer, rapporter, remettre ; *already referred to*, déjà mentionné ; *to refer something to some one (for decision)*, remettre qch. à qn.
refined, cultivé, élégant, poli.
refining, raffinage, m.
refuge, refuge, m. ; *to take refuge*, se réfugier, chercher un refuge.
refuse, refuser (de with infin.), (often rendered by) ne pas vouloir.
regard, regarder, considérer *as = comme*).
regarding, sur, quant à, à l'égard de, ayant trait à ; *regarding it*, en, à ce sujet.

regent, régent,-te ; *Le Régent,* title of the Duc d'Orléans during the minority of Louis XV. (1715-1723.)
region, région, f., pays, m.
register, registre, m.; (in omnibus, etc.) compteur, m.
regret, n., regret, m.; *with an expression of great regret,* avec une expression désolée.
regret, v., regretter.
regular, régulier, en règle, vrai, véritable ; (of physician) diplômé ; *regular places,* places réglementaires, *regular stopping-place,* station, f.
regularity, régularité, f.
regularly, régulièrement.
rehearse, (a play, etc.) répéter.
reign, n., règne, m.; *in the reign of,* sous le règne de.
reign, v., régner ; *to begin to reign,* monter sur le trône.
rein, rêne, f.; *reins of government,* rênes du gouvernement.
rejoice, se réjouir.
relate, raconter.
relationship, parenté, f.
relative, adj., relatif.
relative, n., parent.
release, élargissement, m.
relic, relique, f.
relief, secours, m.
relieve, soulager. adoucir, alléger ; *(my remedy) will relieve you of all that,* vous ôtera tout cela, (fera passer, fera disparaître.)
religious, religieux, de religion ; *religious hypocrite,* hypocrite, faux dévot.
remain, rester, demeurer, subsister.
remaining, dernier, qui reste.
remainder, reste, m.
remains, restes, m. pl., cendres, f. pl.
remark, remarquer ; (say dire ; (to say to one that) faire remarquer à qn. que.
remarkable, remarquable.
remedy, remède, m.

remember, se souvenir (de, que), se rappeler (que).
remove, v.n., déménager, changer de domicile (de... à ; *removed from P. to C.,* quitta P. pour (aller demurer, s'établir, à C.
renaissance, renaissance, f.
render, rendre.
renew, renouveler.
renown, renommée, f.
renowned, renommé (*for*=par).
rent, (of house) loyer, m., (of farm) fermage, m.
reorganize, réorganiser.
repair, réparer, (clothes) raccommoder.
repeat, répéter, redire, réciter ; (say again) répéter, recommencer.
repentance, repentir, m.
replace, (put on again) remettre ; (put in place of, take place of) remplacer.
replant, replanter, planter de nouveau.
reply, n., réponse, f., réplique, f.
reply, v.a., répondre, répliquer.
report, rapport, m. ; (of a meeting, etc.) compte-rendu, m.
represent, représenter, dépeindre.
representation, représentation, f.
representative, n., représentant.
reproach, reprocher(*with, for*=de).
reprove, blâmer.
republic, république, f.
reputation, réputation, f., renommée, f.
request, demande, f., prière, f.
required, demandé.
reside, résider, demeurer.
residence, maison, f., domicile, m., résidence, f. ; (large mansion) hôtel, m.
resign, résigner, se démettre de.
resist, v.n., résister ; v.a., résister à.
resolve, résoudre (de), se décider (à).
resource, ressource, f.
respect, respect, m. [pron. res-pè], égards, m. pl. ; *in all respects,* sous tous les rapports *in this respect,* sous ce rapport.

VOCABULARY. 155

respecting, quant à, pour.

rest, n., (remainder) reste, m., restant, m.; pl. les autres; *the rest of the...*, les autres...

rest, v.n., se reposer; *to rest in or on (a support)* porter sur.

restore, restituer, rendre; rétablir: *was restored to favor*, rentra en grâce; *to restore order*, rétablir l'ordre.

restrain, retenir, contenir, refréner.

result, résultat, m.

resume, reprendre.

retaliate, user de représailles, rendre la pareille.

retinue, suite, f.

retire, se retirer.

retort, riposter, repartir.

retrace, retracer.

retreat, se retirer, battre en retraite.

return, n., retour, m.; *by return of post*, par (le) retour du courrier; *on his return*, à son retour.

return, v.n., (come back) revenir; (go back) retourner; (go or come home) rentrer, (go home) s'en retourner chez soi.

reveal, révéler.

revenue, revenu, m.

reverend, révérend; *the reverend gentleman*, le saint homme.

reverie, rêverie, f.

reverse, revers, m.

revive, faire revivre, rétablir, ressusciter.

revocation, révocation, f.

revolution, révolution, f.

reward, récompense, f., salaire, m.

Rheims, Reims, m.

Rhine, Rhin, m.

Rhone, Rhône, m.

rich, riche, fertile (*in*=en); *the rich*, les riches.

riches, richesse(s), f., biens, m. pl.

richly, richement; *he richly deserves it*, il le mérite bien, il n'a que ce qu'il mérite.

richness, richesse, f., fertilité, f., fécondité, f.

rid of, get, se débarrasser de, se défaire de.

ride, n., promenade (à cheval), f.

ride, v., aller à cheval, monter à cheval, être à cheval; *(in a carriage, etc.)* aller, se promener, être en voiture; *rode by his side*, etc., p. 43, fit marcher son cheval près du sien, (fit route avec lui) sur une certaine distance; *went for a ride*, alla faire une promenade à cheval; *to know how to ride*, savoir monter à cheval.

ridiculous, ridicule, risible, absurde.

riding-whip, cravache, f.

right, adj., bon, qu'il faut, etc.; *you are right*, vous avez raison; *all right*, (c'est) bien! (c'est) bon!

right, n., droit, m.; (hand) droite, f.; *one's rights*, ses droits; *to give (to have) a right to*, donner (avoir) droit à (with nouns), donner (avoir) le droit de (with verbs); *on the right (hand)*, à droite; *on the right of*, à la droite de; *on his right*, à sa droite; *rights of citizenship*, le droit de ●●●

rigor, rigueur, f., sévérité, f.

rim, bord, m.; (of wheel) jante, f.; *outer rim*, bord (extérieur).

ring, n., (in general) anneau, m., rond, m., (for finger) bague, f.

ring, v., sonner.

rise, (pers., sun, moon, etc.), se lever; (figuratively, advance, originate), s'élever; *the blind rose*, le store se souleva; *the sun rose*, le soleil se leva; *he rose to the rank of*, il s'éleva (jusqu') au rang de.

risk, risque, m.; *at the risk of*, au risque de; *to run the risk*, courir (le) risque, risquer.

rival, rival, m.

river, rivière, f.; (large, emptying into the sea) fleuve, m.

road, chemin, m., route, f.; chaussée, f., voie, f.; *the road to X*, le chemin (la route) de X, pour aller à X.

rob, voler, piller, dépouiller; *I have been robbed (of my watch),* on m'a volé (ma montre); *to be robbed of...by....* être dépouillé de...par...

rock, (general) roc, m., roche, f.; (steep and rugged) rocher, m.

rogue, coquin, fripon; (mischievous) farceur.

roll, n., petit pain, m.

roll, v., rouler.

romance, roman, m.

Roman, romain.

romantic, romanesque, romantique (esp. of scenery and of the literary school).

Rome, Rome, f., (pron. with short open *o*).

room, (apartment) chambre, f., salle, f., (in a suite of apartments) pièce, f., (space) place, f.; *his rooms,* son appartement; *to make room for,* faire de la place à.

rope-ladder, échelle de corde, f.

Rouen, m.

rough, rude, (of road) raboteux.

round, adj., rond.

round, prep., autour de; *to go round...,* faire le tour de...

rouse, réveiller.

route, route, f.

row, n., (pers. and things) rang, m., (things only) rangée, f.

row, v., ramer; *I have been rowing a good deal,* j'ai canoté beaucoup, j'ai fait beaucoup de canot; *to go for a row,* aller en canot, (faire une promenade) aller faire une partie de canot.

royal, royal, de (du) roi; *His Royal Highness,* son Altesse royale (abbrev. S. A. R.

rub, frotter.

rubbish, (from excavation, building or demolition) déblais, m. pl., décombres, m. pl.; (literary) fatras, m.

rule, n., règle, f., loi, f.; autorité, f., gouvernement, m.: régime, m.

rule, v., gouverner.

ruler, maître.

rumble, gronder.

run, courir (usually no prep. bef. infin.); *to run after,* courir après, poursuivre; *to run a race (with),* courir, faire une course, lutter de vitesse (avec); *ran and embraced,* courut embrasser; *to run in,* entrer; *to run down the stair,* descendre les escaliers en courant; *to run against,* heurter; *to run the risk,* courir le risque, risquer; *to run a thorn into one's foot,* s'enfoncer une épine dans le pied (la patte, etc.); *came running,* vint en courant.

ruse, ruse, f.

rush, se lancer, s'élancer, se précipiter; *to rush across,* se précipiter dans.

Russia, Russie, f.

Russian, russe, de Russie.

rye, seigle, m.

S.

sack, sac, m.

sacrament, sacrement, m.

sad, triste, déplorable.

saddle, n., selle, f., (as part of harness) sellette, f.

saddle, v., seller.

sail, n., voile, f.; *to set sail,* faire voile, mettre à la voile.

sail, v., faire voile, appareiller; *to sail up,* remonter.

sailing, adj., à voiles.

sailor, marin, matelot.

saint, saint; in naming saints, *saint* has no capital or hyphen in French, as it has when used in names of saints' days, places and churches. (See examples below).

St. Andrew, saint André.

St. Benoît, saint Benoît.

St. Denis, saint Denis, (church and town Saint-Denis).

St. Helena, Sainte-Hélène.

St. Lawrence, Saint-Laurent, m.; *The River St. L.,* le (fleuve) Saint-Laurent; *The Gulf of St. L.,* le golfe du Saint-Laurent.

Saint Louis, saint Louis.

Saint Malo, Saint-Malo.

St. Paul, saint Paul; *St. Paul's,* Saint-Paul de Londres, m.
St. Peter, saint Pierre; *in St. Peter's (church),* à Saint-Pierre de Rome, m.
St. Petersburg, (Saint-)Pétersbourg.
St. Remi, saint Remi.
Salian, salien; *Salian Francs,* Francs saliens.
salute, saluer.
same, même; *at the same time,* en même temps.
sand, sable, m.
sardine, sardine, f.
satire, satire, f.
satisfy, contenter, satisfaire; *satisfied with,* satisfait (content) de.
savage, sauvage.
save, sauver.
saving. adj., économe.
Savoy, Savoie, f.
Saxe-Coburg-Gotha, Saxe-Cobourg-Gotha.
say, dire, parler; *to say to oneself,* se dire; *it is said that,* on dit que; *that is to say,* c'est-à-dire; *you have only to say so,* (see under "only,"); *he is said to have gone,* on dit qu'il alla; *so saying,* à ces mots; *it may be said to have had,* on pourrait dire qu'elle a eu.
saying, mot, m., dicton, m.
scald, échauder.
scale, échelle, f.
scamper off, s'enfuir, se sauver, décamper, détaler.
scandal, scandale, m., médisance, f.; *School for Scandal,* École de médisance.
scarcely, à peine; *scarcely... when,* à peine...que, pas plus tôt ...que
scare, v., effrayer, épouvanter; n. (fright) peur, f., frayeur, f.
scatter, disperser, éparpiller, disséminer.
scholar, écolier; (learned man, etc.) savant, érudit.
scholarly, savant, érudit.
school, école, f.

school-report, rapport de fin de mois, m.; (quarterly) bulletin trimestriel, m.
science, science, f.
scientific, scientifique; (of instruments) de précision.
scorch, brûler.
score, vingtaine, f.
Scotland, Écosse, f.
scrap, morceau, m., bout, m., bribe, f., (bribes pl. in sense of *snatches, quotations*); (paper) chiffon, m.
scruple, scrupule, m.
scurvy, scorbut, m.
sea, mer, f., océan, m.; *to fall into the sea,* tomber à la mer.
seaman, marin, homme de mer.
seaport, port de mer, m.
search, n., recherche, f.; *in search of,* à la recherche de, cherchant.
search, v., chercher, fouiller.
sea-side, bord de la mer, m. (*at the*=au.)
seat, siège, m., (long) banc, m.; (space for one in travelling) place, f.; p. 108. *seats for two,* places pour deux.
seat, v.a., asseoir, faire asseoir; *to be seated (sitting)* être assis.
second, adj., second, deuxième; (of kings, dates, etc.) deux; *second-class,* adj., de deuxième (classe); *Second Empire,* Second Empire.
second, n., seconde, f.
secret, secret, m.
secretary, secrétaire, m.
sect, secte, f.
secure, assurer, (*for*=à.)
see, voir, remarquer; *to see again,* revoir; *to go to see,* aller voir; *saw him coming,* le vit qui venait, qui se dirigeait; *as I had seen the blacksmith do,* comme je l'avais vu faire au (par le) forgeron, maréchal (ferrant).
seek, chercher (à before infin.)
seem, sembler, paraître, avoir l'air; (*il semble* generally takes the subjunct. after it, *il me semble,* the indicat.)

Seignior, seigneur.
Seine, f.
seize, saisir, s'emparer de.
self-sufficiency, suffisance, f.
sell, vendre ; *to sell again,* revendre.
senate, sénat, m.
send, envoyer, adresser ; *to send off (pers. or things),* expédier ; *to send hastily (a person),* dépêcher (un courrier, etc.); *to send for,* envoyer chercher, faire venir, (persons only, as doctor, etc.) appeler ; *(a physician) being sent for by,* étant appelé par.
sense, sens, m. ; (good sense) bon sens, sens commun.
sensible, (to the senses) sensible, (wise) sensé, sage, de bon sens ; *a most sensible woman,* une femme des plus sensées.
sensibly, (relating to the senses) sensiblement ; (wisely) sensément, raisonnablement, sagement.
sentence, (gram.) phrase, f. ; (of court) sentence, f.; (maxim) sentence, maxime, f.
sentiment, sentiment, m.
sentry, sentinelle, f.; factionnaire, m.
separate, séparer.
September, septembre, m.
sequel, suite, f.
series, série, f., suite, f.
serious, sérieux.
sermon, sermon, m.
servant, serviteur, servante; (for house) domestique, m. and f., bonne, f. ; (officer's servant) brosseur.
serve, servir ; *to serve as,* servir de ; *to serve to* (w. infin.), servir à ; *had served his brother,* avait été au service de son frère ; *trained to serve you,* dressées à ton service.
service, service, m.; (church) office, m., service (divin), m. ; *to do (render) a service to,* rendre service à.
set, n., série, f., collection, f., etc. ; *set of apartments,* appartement, m., sing.
set, v., placer, mettre, poser, fixer ; *to set fire to,* mettre le feu à ; (houses, forests, etc., on large scale) incendier ; *to set free,* mettre en liberté, élargir ; *to set sail for,* mettre à la voile (faire voile) pour ; *to set out for,* partir pour ; *to set out again,* repartir.
settle, (alight) s'asseoir, se poser, s'abattre.
settlement, établissement, m., colonisation, f.
settler, colon.
seven, sept ; *seventh,* septième, (of kings, dates, etc.) sept.
Seven Years' War, guerre de sept ans, f.
seventeen, dix-sept.
seventy, soixante-dix.
several, plusieurs.
severe, sévère.
severely, sévèrement.
severity, sévérité, f., rigueur, f.
sew, coudre.
shaft, (machinery) arbre, m. ; (of vehicle) brancard, m.
shake, secouer, agiter.
shall, as simple sign of future, needs no further translation ; but when implying will or determination, *vouloir* and *falloir* are often used as equivalents ; *he shall go,* il faut, je veux qu'il aille, *shall I go?,* voulez-vous que j'aille ? *where shall I begin?,* (par où voulez-vous (faut il) que je commence ?
shame, honte, f.; *with shame,* de honte.
shanty, (in American woods) chantier, m.
shape, n., forme, f., coupe, f.
shape, v., former, façonner, modeler ; *I shaped it to the foot,* je l'ajustai au pied (sabot).
sharpen, aiguiser, affiler.
sharply, vivement, sévèrement.
shave, raser, faire la barbe (à).
she, elle.
she-ass, ânesse, bourrique.
shed, hangar, m., appentis, m.
sheep, mouton, m., brebis, f.
sheet, drap, m.
shine, luire, briller.

VOCABULARY. 159

shingle, (pebbles) galet, m., (sometimes plur.); (of wood) bardeau, m.

ship, bâtiment, m., navire, m., (war) vaisseau, m., (ironclad) cuirassé, m.

ship-building, construction de vaisseaux, f.

ship-yard, chantier, m.

shoe, n., soulier, m.; (horse-shoe) fer de cheval, m.

shoe, v., (pers.) chausser; (horse) ferrer.

shop, boutique, f.; magasin, m.; (work-shop) atelier, m.; (blacksmith's shop) forge, f.

shore, (sea) rivage, m., bord, m.; (river) bord, m., rive, f., rivage, m.

short, court; *in short,* (bref); *(in) a short time,* (en) peu de temps, (=shortly, soon), sous peu, bientôt; *to make a head shorter,* faire plus court de la tête, raccourcir de la tête.

shortly, bientôt.

should, when not a mere sign of tense, as in *if he should go.*=s'il allait, *I should be glad.*=je serais content, can generally be rendered by devoir (especially in pres. indic. and conditional), il faut (with subjunct.); *you should not laugh,* il ne faut pas rire; *you should have seen him,* il fallait le voir (in either sense of the words).

shoulder, épaule, f.

show, montrer, faire voir, démontrer, indiquer, déployer.

shower, averse, f., ondée, f.

shut, fermer; *to shut again* (after opening or coming in) refermer; *to shut oneself in,* se renfermer.

shy, adj., timide, farouche.

shy, v., faire un écart, se jeter de côté.

sick, (ill) malade; *to be sick* (from nausea), avoir mal au cœur.

sickness, (illness) maladie, f., (nausea) mal de cœur, m., (sea-sickness) mal de mer; *about his sickness,* sur sa maladie.

side, côté, m.; (of mountain) côte, f., pente, f., (of mountain chains) versant, m., (bank of river) rive, f.; *at his side,* à côté de lui.

sidewalk, trottoir, m.

siege, siège, m.

sigh, soupirer (*for*=après).

sign, signe, m.; (sign-board) enseigne, f.; (notice) écriteau, m.; (plate) plaque, f., p. 109.

signal, signal, m. (*for*=de).

silence, silence, m.

silent, silencieux; *to be, become silent,* se taire; *had remained very silent,* était resté (avait écouté) sans parler.

silk, n., soie, f., adj., en (de) soie; *silk culture,* sériciculture, f., culture de la soie, f.

silk-worm, ver à soie, m.

silly, sot, niais, naïf.

silver, n., argent, m.; adj., d'argent, en argent.

similar, semblable, pareil, analogue.

simple, simple; (foolish) simple, niais, naïf, bon.

since, prep. and adv., depuis; *some time since,* il y a quelque temps; conj., (time) depuis que, (reason) puisque, comme.

sincere, sincère.

sing, chanter.

single, seul; *to eat at a single mouthful,* n'en faire qu'une bouchée.

Sir, (in address) monsieur; (as a title, not to be translated) Sir....

sister, sœur.

sit, s'asseoir, (be seated) être assis; se poser, se placer; (of an assembly) siéger; *sitting,* assis; *to sit, as to stand,* is often rendered by the verb *se tenir,* (see "stand"): *sat in ill-natured silence,* gardait un silence rechigné; *he sits behind the counter,* il se tient derrière le bureau.

site, emplacement, m.

situated, situé, placé; *situated a league from,* (situé) à une lieue de.

six, six.

sixteen, seize; *sixteenth,* seizième (kings, dates, etc.) seize.

sixty, soixante.

size, grosseur, f.; grandeur, f., importance, f., (person) taille, f.; *of extraordinary size*, d'une grosseur extraordinaire, énorme.
sketch, esquisse, f., étude, f.
skilful, habile, adroit, industrieux.
skin, peau, f.
skull, crâne, m.
sky, ciel, m.
slanderer, médisant, calomniateur.
slay, tuer.
sleep, dormir.
sleeping-room, chambre à coucher, f.
slender, (stem) mince, (pers.) svelte.
slip, glisser; *slipped down from*, se laissa glisser de; *slipped out*, p. 49, descendit furtivement, se glissa à terre; *to let slip*, laisser échapper.
small, petit.
smell, sentir; *to smell bad, strong*, sentir mauvais, fort; *to smell good*, sentir bon.
smile, n., souris, m., sourire, m.
smile, v., sourire, rire.
smith, forgeron, m., (shoeing-smith) maréchal ferrant, m.
smithy, forge, f.
sneer, rire moqueur, m., air de méprise, m., ricanement, m.
snow-drop, perce-neige, m.
snuff, n., tabac (à priser) m.; *pinch of snuff*, prise de tabac; *to take snuff*, priser.
snuff-box, tabatière, f.
so, adv., si, ainsi, comme cela, de cette manière (façon); often rendered by *le* as the object of the verb; (beginning a clause) ainsi, aussi, (after verb in French clause) donc; *so much*, tant; *so it was done*, ainsi fut fait, (ainsi dit, ainsi fait); *so I started the fire*, j'allumai donc le feu; *to say so, think so, do so*, le dire, le croire, le faire; *why so?*, pourquoi donc? *so saying*, en disant cela, à ces mots; *so that*, de sorte que; pour que, afin que; *so as (not) to*, de manière à 'ne pas'.

soap, savon, m.
social, social.
socialist, socialiste.
society, société, f., monde, m.
sofa, canapé, m., sofa, m.
soil, sol, m., terre, f., terroir, m.
soldier, soldat, m.
some, adj., quelque(s); du, de la, des; pron. quelques-uns, en; *some day*, un jour (ou l'autre); *there were still some*, il y en avait encore.
somebody, quelqu'un.
something, quelque chose, m.; *looked for something to eat*, cherchait de quoi manger.
sometimes, quelque fois, parfois.
somewhat, un peu, quelque peu; assez; *somewhat similar*, à peu près semblable.
somewhere, quelque part; *somewhere else*, ailleurs, autre part.
son, fils.
song, chanson, f., (of bird) chant. m., ramage, m.
songster, chanteur, chantre.
soon, bientôt; *as soon as*, dès que, aussitôt que, à peine...que; *no sooner...than*, à peine...que, pas plus tôt...que.
Sorbonne, f.; *doctors of the S.*, docteurs de Sorbonne.
sorceress, sorcière.
sorrow, tristesse, f., chagrin, m., douleur, f.; *sorrows*, p. 78, malheurs, m- pl.
sorry, fâché, désolé; *he was soon sorry for being*, il se repentit bientôt d'avoir été; *I am sorry that*, je regrette que (with subjunct.)
sort, sorte, f., espèce, f.; *all sorts of*, toute(s) sorte(s) de.
sou, sou, m.
soup, potage, m., soupe, f., bouillon, m.
source, source, f.
south, sud, m., midi, m.; adj., sud, du sud, du midi, méridional; *in the south of France*, dans le midi (de la F.); *the south coast*, la côte sud.

southern, du sud, du midi, méridional; *the southern side*, la rive sud.

sovereign, souverain, m.

sow, (seed) semer; (ground) ensemencer.

space, espace, m.; *how small a space*, combien (quel) peu d'espace.

Spain, Espagne, f.

Spaniard, Espagnol.

Spanish, espagnol, d'Espagne.

spark, étincelle, f.; (not brilliant) lueur, f.

speak, v.n., parler; v.a., parler, prononcer, dire; *to speak aloud*, parler, prononcer tout haut.

spectator, spectateur, assistant, m.

speech, (faculty) parole, f., langage, m.; (address) discours, m., (short) allocution, f.

spend, dépenser; (of time) passer.

spin, filer.

spirit, esprit, m.; (soul) âme, f.

spirited, plein de vigueur, de courage, etc.; (horses) fougueux, vif.

spiritual, spirituel; *spiritual aid*, secours religieux.

spite, n., dépit, m.; *in spite of*, malgré, en dépit de.

spite, v., contrarier, faire enrager.

splash-board, garde-crotte, m.

splendid, splendide, magnifique.

spoil, gâter, détruire.

spoke, rais, m., rayon, m.

sport, sport, m., jeu, m., divertissement, m.; *some fine sport*, une bonne farce, quelque chose de drôle.

spot, tache, f.; (place) endroit, lieu; *at that spot*, à (dans) cet endroit.

spread, étendre, répandre; p. 103, disséminer.

spring, n., printemps, m.; *in spring*, au printemps, (of carriage, etc.) ressort, m.; *with springs*, suspendu.

spring, v.n., (grow) pousser; (leap) sauter, bondir.

spruce, (in Canada) épinette, f., especially *the white spruce*, épinette blanche.

spur, éperon, m.

squadron, (mil.) escadron, m.; (nav.) escadre, f.

square, adj., carré.

square, n., (public) place, f.

squirrel, écureuil, m.

stab, poignarder, frapper d'un coup de poignard.

stage, scène, f., théâtre, m.

stage-box, avant-scène, f.

stage-coach, diligence, f., voiture publique, f.; *in a stage-coach*, en diligence.

stair, escalier, m.; *up-stairs*, en haut; *to come down stairs*, descendre (l'escalier).

stair-case, cage d'escalier, f., escalier, m.

stairway, escalier, m.

stake, poteau, m., pieu, m.; *to be burned at the stake (lit. on the pile)*, monter, mourir sur le bûcher.

stand, v., (erect) être (se tenir) debout; se tenir, se trouver; être placé, situé; this verb, like some others, as *sit*, *lie*, has often no equivalent in French, and must be replaced by some word of general signification; *a sentry stood there*, une sentinelle (un factionnaire) se tenait (se trouvait) là; *stand back!* arrière! reculez!

standing, position, f., rang, m.; *standing in society*, position sociale.

star, étoile, f.

start, v.a., faire partir, mettre en marche; v.n., partir, se mettre en route, (on *a voyage*, pour un voyage); *to start a fire*, faire du feu, allumer du feu (*the fire*, le feu).

state, état, m., condition, f.; adj., d'état; *United States*, Etats-Unis, m. pl.; *state secret*, secret d'état, m.

stately, imposant, majestueux.

statesman, homme d'état, politique.

station, station, f., (large railway station) gare, f.

statue, statue, f.

stay, n., séjour, m.

stay, v., rester, demeurer, séjourner.

stead, lieu, m., place, f.; *to stand one in good stead*, être d'une grande utilité à qn., rendre de grands services à qn.

steam, vapeur, f.; *to go by steam*, aller à la vapeur.

steam-engine, machine à vapeur, f.

steamer, (bateau à) vapeur, m.; (large ocean steamer, often) paquebot, m.; *Atlantic steamer*, transatlantique, m.

stem, tige, f.

step, n., pas, m.; (of a stair) marche, f., degré, m.; (of a vehicle) marchepied, m.

step, v., faire un pas; (tread) marcher (on=sur); *to step in*, entrer; *to step forward*, avancer.

steward, (house) maître d'hôtel, (land) régisseur; (director, manager) intendant.

stifling, étouffant.

still, adj., tranquille, calme; *keep still*, restez tranquille(s), taisez-vous.

still, adv., encore, toujours; *still greater*, encore plus grand.

sting, piquer.

stirrup, étrier, m.

stocks, fonds publics, m.

stoop, se baisser; *to stoop and pick it up*, qu'on se baisse pour le ramasser.

stop, v.a., arrêter; v.n., s'arrêter; *he stops eating*, il cesse de manger.

storm, orage, m., tempête, f.

story, histoire, f., conte, m., (house) étage; *in the fourth story*, au quatrième; *second story window*, fenêtre du deuxième (étage); *a story is told of B. that*, on raconte de B. que.

straight, adj., droit; adv., droit, tout droit, directement; *leading straight forward*, qui va tout droit.

strait, détroit, m.; *The Straits of* ...le Détroit de...; *The Straits of Dover*, le Pas de Calais.

straiten, rétrécir; *in straitened circumstances*, dans la gêne.

strange, étrange, singulier, bizarre, extraordinaire.

stranger, étranger, inconnu, nouveau-venu, nouvel-arrivant.

strangle, étrangler.

Strasburg, Strasbourg, m., (sometimes f.)

straw, paille, f.

stream, courant, m.; *to flow in a full stream (be full to the brim)*, couler à pleins bords.

street, rue, f.; *in (on) the street*, dans la rue; *along the streets*, dans, par les rues.

strength, force, f., forces, f. pl.

stretch, étendre.

strike, frapper; *to strike out (a name, etc.)*, rayer, raturer, biffer, effacer.

striking, frappant, remarquable.

strip, déshabiller, *strip bark off, strip....of bark*, écorcer.

strong, fort, vigoureux; (of materials) dur, résistant.

strongly, fortement, profondément.

struggle, n., lutte, f.

struggle, v., lutter (with=contre).

student, étudiant; *student of (in) law, medicine, etc.*, étudiant en droit, en médecine, etc.

studio, atelier, m.

study, n., étude, f., travail, m.; *for study*, pour étudier.

study, v., étudier, faire ses études, travailler; *to study law*, faire son droit.

stuff, bourrer (with=de); (cookery) farcir (de).

stupid, bête, sot, stupide.

style, style, m.; (fashionable) train, m.

subject, sujet, m., matière, f., fonds, m.; *to have for its subject*, avoir pour sujet.

subsequent, subséquent (not often used in French); *its subsequent history*, la suite de l'histoire de ce tableau; *his subsequent life*, la suite de sa vie.

succeed, v.n., réussir ; v.a., (follow) succéder à ; *succeeding*, qui suit, suivant.

success, succès, m., réussite, f.

successful, heureux.

such, adj., tel (before the noun), pareil (after the noun) ; *such a message,* un message pareil ; *not such a fool as,* pas si bête (sot) que ; *don't be in such a hurry,* ne vous pressez pas tant, rien ne presse ; *such as...*, tel(s) que, comme, on p. 57, omit in translation *such things as* ; adv., si, tellement ; *such great progress,* tant de progrès ; *with such violence,* avec une telle violence, tant de violence ; *such a favorite with,* si grand favori (à tel point favori) de.

suddenly, subitement, soudainement, tout à coup.

suffer, souffrir (*from*=de) ; (a defeat), subir ; *suffered great persecution,* furent victimes d'une grande persécution.

sugar, sucre, m. ; *maple sugar,* sucre d'érable ; *cane sugar,* sucre de canne.

sugar-beet, betterave, f.

sugar-maple, érable à sucre, m., érable du Canada.

suite, suite, f. ; *suite of apartments,* appartement, m.

sum, somme, f.

summon, (call together) convoquer, (send for) appeler.

sun, soleil, m.

Sunday, dimanche, m.

sunshine, clarté du soleil, f. (weather) beau temps, m.

supper, souper, m.

supply, n., provision, f., approvisionnement, m.

supply, v., fournir.

support, supporter, soutenir, nourrir.

suppose, supposer, on p. 88 followed by indic. ; *supposed to be,* supposé (censé) être.

sure, sûr, certain ; *to be sure!*, mais oui, sans doute ; (at the end of a clause = *of course*) bien entendu, naturellement.

surgeon, chirurgien.

surname, surnom, m.

surnamed, surnommé.

surpass, surpasser, exceller.

surprise, surprise, f., étonnement, m. ; *expressed surprise at being,* trans. *said he was surprised,* etc. (see under "surprised.")

surprised (at), surpris, étonné (de with infin., *que* with subjunct., *de ce que* with indic.) ; *surprised at being called in,* surpris de ce qu'on l'avait appelé.

surrender, v.a., rendre ; v.n., se rendre.

surround, entourer, environner.

suspect, soupçonner, se douter de, se défier (se méfier) de ; *suspected,* soupçonné.

swallow, avaler.

swear, jurer (de with infin.), prêter serment.

sweetmeats, sucreries, f.pl. ; bonbons, m. pl.

swim, nager.

Switzerland, Suisse, f.

sycamore, sycomore, m.

sympathy, sympathie, f., part, f.

system, système, m.

T.

table, table, f.

tailor, tailleur.

take, prendre ; *to take off*, ôter, enlever ; *to take up,* ramasser, lever ; *let them take,* que (l')on prenne ; *to take (away) with one,* emporter, emmener ; *to take care of something,* prendre (avoir) soin de qch., conserver qch., *of some one,* soigner ; *to take care to,* avoir soin de ; *to take care not to,* prendre garde de, se garder de ; *to take the air,* prendre l'air ; *to take flight,* (of birds) prendre son vol, sa volée ; *to take a look at it,* y voir ; *to take breath,* respirer, reprendre haleine ; *to take place,* avoir lieu, se faire, se passer ; *to take part (in),* prendre part (à) ; *to take one's place,* prendre sa place, p. 110 l. 6, monter en voiture ; *being taken*

ill, étant tombé malade; *he was taken to see*, on lui fit visiter, on le mena voir; *to take the liberty of*, se permettre de, prendre la liberté de; *to take (one) for (the other)*, prendre pour, regarder comme, croire; *to take...from his pocket, the table*, prendre...dans sa poche, sur la table, see p. 67, note; *to take it as*, le prendre comme, y voir (trouver), voir en cela; *to take from (its frame)*, ôter; *here, take it*, tenez, le voilà; *to take one prisoner*, faire qu. prisonnier, prendre; *to take into one's own hands*, prendre dans ses (propres) mains, en main; *to take possession of*, prendre possession de.

tale, conte, m., récit, m., histoire, f.; *fairy tale*, conte de fées.

talent, talent, m., *man of talent*, homme de talent.

talented, plein de talent.

talk, parler, causer.

tamarac, (larch) épinette rouge, f.

tan, v. tanner.

tan-bark, tan, m., écorce à tan, f.

task, tâche, f., travail, m., ouvrage, m., besogne. f. ; *to take to task*, prendre à partie, gronder, sermonner, reprocher.

tassel, gland, m.

taste, goût, m.; p. 85 *a taste for*, etc., le goût de la littérature, et aussi celui des sciences.

tax, impôt, m., contributions, f. pl.

tax-gatherer, percepteur des contributions; (in ancient history, or disparagingly) publicain.

teach, apprendre, enseigner, (à before infin.)

teapot, théière, f.

tear, n., larme, f.; (pl.) larmes, pleurs, m.

tear, v., déchirer; *tear out, off, away*, arracher.

tease, taquiner.

telegraph, n., télégraphe, m.; adj., télégraphique, de télégraphe; *telephone*, téléphone, m.

tell, dire, (a story) raconter; *he was heard telling*, on l'entendit qui disait; *to tell the time*, savoir l'heure; *why did'nt she tell me so at first?*, pourquoi n'a-t-elle pas commencé par me le dire?

temper, caractère, m., humeur, f.

tempt, tenter (*to*=de).

ten, dix; *ten cents*, dix sous.

tender, tendre.

term, terme, m., (university) semestre, m., année scolaire, f.

terrible, terrible, affreux.

terrify, épouvanter, effrayer, frapper de terreur.

territory, territoire, m.

terror, terreur, f., effroi, m.; *in terror*, avec terreur, effroi.

thaler, thaler, taler, m.

than, que, de; *more than*, plus que, (before numbers) plus de.

thank, remercier; *thank you, merci*; *thank Heaven!*, Dieu merci.

thanks, remerciements *or* remerciments, m. pl.

that, those, adj., ce, cette, ces.

that, those, pron., ce, cela, celui, celle, ceux, celles; *those who*, ceux qui; *that is the difference*, c'est là la différence; *is that you?*, est-ce vous? (pop. c'est-y vous?); p. 61. *that is, to fasten*, c'est d'attacher.

that, conj., que; (so) *that*, pour que, afin que, de sorte que; *that I may know*, pour que je le sache.

thatched with, couvert de.

the, le, la, les.

theatre, théâtre, m., spectacle, m.

theft, vol, m.

their, leur, leurs; *theirs*, le leur, etc.; à eux, à elles.

them, les, leur, eux; *of them*, d'eux, en.

then, alors, ensuite, puis; donc; *but then*, mais (alors).

theology, théologie, f.

theological, théologique.

there, là, y; *up there, down there, in there*, là-haut, là-bas, là-dedans; *thereupon*, là-dessus; *there is, are*, il y a, (with emphasis upon there) voilà; *there was once (upon a time)*, il y avait (il était) une fois.

therefore, donc, aussi, par conséquent.

they, ils, eux, elles; (indefinitely) on; (impersonally in French before *être*) ce ; p. 25, *that they were mad,* que c'étaient elles qui l'étaient.

thief, voleur.

thing, chose, f., objet, m., affaire, f.; on p. 57, omit translation of *such things as.*

think, penser, croire; *I think so,* je le crois, je crois que oui ; *to think of,* penser à (when v.n.), de (when v.a.); *what are you thinking of?,* à quoi pensez-vous ? ; *what do you think of it?,* qu'en pensez-vous ? ; *what do you think of this view?,* comment trouvez-vous ce coup d'œil ? ; *he thinks it pretty,* il le trouve joli ; *I thought I would tell you,* j'ai eu l'idée de vous le dire; *to think fit to,* juger à propos de, trouver bon de ; *wished to be thought...,* voulait passer pour..., voulait qu'on la crût (trouvât)...

third, troisième, (kings, dates, etc.) trois.

thirst, soif, f.

thirsty, altéré.

thirteen, treize; *thirteenth,* treizième, (kings, dates, etc.) treize.

thirty, trente ; *thirtieth,* trentième, (of kings, dates, etc.) trente.

this, these, adj., ce, cet, cette, ces.

this, these, pron., ce, celui, celle, ceux, celles ; ceci, cela; p. 41, *she did this,* elle y parvint, arriva ; *on this,* là-dessus, sur quoi ; *this is one of them,* en voici un ; *this was done,* ainsi fut fait, ce qui fut dit fut fait.

thither, là, y.

thorn, épine, f.

though, quoique, bien que.

thought, pensée, f.

thoughtfully, d'un air pensif.

thoughtless, thoughtless fellow, étourdi.

thousand, mille ; (in dates, when the first word, followed by other numbers) mil.

thousandth, millième.

threaten, menacer.

three, trois.

Three Rivers, Trois-Rivières.

thrive, (of plants) profiter, venir bien.

throat, gorge, f.

throne, trône, m.

through, à travers, au travers de, par ; *through the streets, the town,* par les rues, par la ville ; *through his rooms,* dans son appartement ; *to speak through one's nose,* parler du nez.

throughout, partout, dans tout, d'un bout à l'autre, dans toute l'étendue de.

throw, jeter, lancer, (a rider) démonter ; *to throw open,* ouvrir ; *to throw away,* jeter ; *threw him into the ditch,* l'a jeté dans le fossé.

thunder, tonnère, m ; *thunder bolt,* foudre, f.

thus, ainsi, comme (il) suit.

ticket, billet, m., (numbered ticket is often) numéro, m.

tide, marée, f.; flux et reflux de la mer, m.

tightly, étroitment.

till, prep., jusqu'à; conj., jusqu'à ce que ; *not...till,* ne...pas...avant (avant que).

timber, bois de construction, m.

time, temps, m. ; (occasion, repetition) fois, f.; (hour of day) heure, f.; *every time,* chaque fois, toutes les fois ; *at the time when,* à l'instant où, au moment où (que) ; *at another time,* une autre fois ; *what time is it?,* quelle heure est-il ? ; *it is high time,* il est grand temps (followed by subjunct. or infin.); *to have time to,* avoir le temps de ; *in the time of J. M.,* du temps de J. M.; *in modern times,* dans les temps modernes ; *in those times,* dans ce temps-là ; *at that time,* à cette époque ; *some time ago,* il y a quelque temps ; *for a time,* pendant un certain temps ; *from this time on,* à partir de cette époque ; *in time,* à temps ; p. 87, au bout de quelque temps.

tire, (of wheel) bande, f., bandage, m.

tithe, dîme, f.
title, titre, m.
to, à, de; pour, afin de; jusqu'à; *to France,* en France; *to America,* en Amérique; *to Canada,* au Canada; *to Palestine,* en Palestine; *as if to,* comme pour.
toast, rôtir, faire griller; *toasted cheese,* fromage grillé.
tobacco, tabac, m.
to-day, aujourd'hui; (at present) de nos jours, actuellement.
together, ensemble.
toil, travailler (fort), peiner, se donner du mal.
tolerance, tolérance, f.
tolerant, tolérant.
tomb, (generally simple, plain) tombe, f., (elevated, etc.) tombeau, m.
to-morrow, demain.
tone, ton, m.; *in a tone of,* d'un ton de.
tongue, langue, f.
tonsure, tonsure, f.
too, trop; (as well) aussi, également; *too much,* trop (de); *too early,* trop tôt, de trop bonne heure.
tool, outil, m., instrument, m.
tooth, dent, f.
top, haut, m., sommet, m., dessus, m., (of tree) cime, f., faîte, m., (of omnibus, diligence, etc.) impériale, f. (on p. 110, use *dessus* in the first two cases only).
touch, toucher.
touching, touchant, émouvant.
toward(s), vers, (fig.) envers.
town, ville, f. (except after *en,* the article is not omitted in French as in English before *town*).
trace, trace, f.; (in harness) trait, m.
trade, commerce, m.; métier, m.; p. 100, industrie, f.; *fur trade,* pelleterie, f., commerce des pelleteries.
trading, commerce, m.
tragedy, drame, m., tragédie, f.
tragic, tragique; *a tragic poet,* un (poète) tragique.
train, n., train, m.

train, v., dresser, former; *once they are trained to...,* une fois dressées à.
tram-car, voiture de tramway, f. (but the word in general use for the vehicle itself is simply *tramway, m.*)
tram line, ligne de tramways, f.
tramway, tramway, m., ligne de tramways.
transfer-ticket, correspondance, f.
translate, traduire.
translator, traducteur.
trap, (fig.) piège, m.; (mouse trap) souricière, f.
travel, n., voyage, m.; *G's Travels,* les Voyages de G.
travel, v., voyager; *travel over,* parcourir.
traveller, voyageur; *commercial traveller,* commis voyageur.
treat, traiter; *to treat well,* traiter bien.
treatise, traité, m.
treaty, traité, m.
tree, arbre, m.
tremble, trembler; *to run trembling,* courir tout tremblant.
tribe, tribu, f.
trick, tour, m.; *to play him a trick,* lui jouer un tour, lui faire une niche.
trifle, bagatelle, f., rien, m.; *a trifle too strong,* (famil.) un (tout) petit peu trop fort.
trifling, insignifiant, léger, petit; *trifling oversights,* petites négligences.
trim, tailler.
triumph, n., triomphe, m.
triumph, v., triompher; *triumph over,* triompher de.
troop, troupe, f.; *troops* (soldiers), troupes, f.pl.
trot, trotter.
trouble, peine, f., chagrin, m.; pl. ennuis, m., chagrins, m.
troublesome, ennuyeux, gênant, embarrassant.
troupe, troupe, f.

trousers, pantalon, m. sing.; *a pair of trousers*, un pantalon.
true, vrai, véritable, réel; *true, madam*, c'est vrai, madame.
truffle, truffe, f.
truly, vraiment, véritablement; (beginning a sentence) en vérité; *no, truly*, non certes, ma foi non.
trundle, rouler, (see under "pick up").
truth, vérité, f.; *to tell the truth*, à vrai dire.
try, essayer, tâcher, s'efforcer, (*to*=de); (prisoner, accused) mettre en jugement; *to try and find out*, tâcher de savoir.
tub, cuve, f., (for washing) cuvier, m.
turkey, dinde, m. and f. is the general term, although there is a separate masc. form, *dindon*.
turn, n., tour, m.; *in his turn*, à son tour; *by turns, in turn*, tour à tour, (sometimes of several persons) à tour de rôle.
turn, v.n., tourner, se tourner, se retourner; v.a., tourner; *to turn round*, se (re)tourner; *he turned to me*, il se (re)tourna vers moi; *to turn a deaf ear*, see "deaf."
tutor, précepteur, (college) répétiteur.
twelve, douze; *twelve o'clock*, midi, m.; *twelve o'clock at night*, minuit, m.; *twelfth*, douzième, (kings, dates, etc.) douze.
twenty, vingt; *twentieth*, vingtième, (dates) vingt.
twice, deux fois.
two, deux.
two-horse, adj., à deux chevaux.

U.

ugly, laid, vilain.
umbrella, parapluie, m.
unable, incapable, hors d'état (de); *to be unable to*, ne pas pouvoir, ne pas savoir, ne pas parvenir à.

unaffected, simple, sans affectation.
uncle, oncle; *an uncle of his*, un de ses oncles, (famil.) un sien oncle.
under, sous, au-dessous de; *under ordinary circumstances*, dans des circonstances ordinaires; *under obligation*, see "obligation"; *under ground*, sous terre.
undergo, subir.
understand, comprendre, entendre; *to make oneself understood*, se faire comprendre.
undertake, entreprendre, se charger de.
undertone, in an, à mi-voix, à voix basse.
undress, v.n., se déshabiller.
undue, excessif; *to take undue advantage of*, abuser de.
uneasy, inquiet, mal à son aise; *don't be uneasy*, soyez tranquille, ne vous inquiétez pas de cela.
unfortunately, malheureusement, par malheur.
ungrateful, ingrat; *very ungrateful in (of) C*, très ingrat à C.
unhappy, malheureux.
unharness, déharnacher, ôter le harnais.
uniform, adj., uniforme, uni.
uniform, n., uniforme, m.
unimportant, insignifiant, peu important, sans importance.
unite, unir, réunir.
united, uni; *United States*, États-Unis, m. pl.
universal, universel.
university, université, f.
unless, à moins que...ne (with subjunct.), à moins de (with infin.)
unlikely, improbable, peu probable, invraisemblable.
unpleasant, désagréable; (odor) mauvais.
unpunished, impuni.
until, prep., jusqu'à; conj., jusqu'à ce que.
unwilling, peu disposé; *to be unwilling*, ne pas vouloir.

up, en haut, au haut : (out of bed) levé; *you are up (the hill),* vous voilà arrivés (au sommet) ; *to cut up,* découper ; *to be well up in a subject,* see "well."
upon, sur ; *to live upon,* vivre de.
upper, supérieur.
upright, droit.
us, nous.
use, n., usage, m., avantage, m.; *to be of use,* servir (à) ; *what use is it to him?,* à quoi lui sert-il ? ; *was not of much use* (p. 44), ne disait pas grand' chose ; *to make a right use of,* faire un bon usage (emploi) de, employer bien.
use, v.n., avoir coutume, avoir l'habitude ; often rendered by the simple impf. indic.; v.a., se servir de, employer ; *it is used as,* il sert de, est employé comme.
useful, utile ; *to be useful to him,* lui profiter.
useless, inutile.
usual, ordinaire, habituel, accoutumé, usuel, (of words, etc.) usité ; *as usual,* (comme) à l'ordinaire, comme d'habitude ; *in the usual form,* dans les formes, la forme usuelle ; *later than usual,* plus tard que de coutume, d'habitude.
usually, ordinairement, d'ordinaire.
Utopia, Utopie, f. (also a common noun, as in English).
utter, énoncer, prononcer, émettre, pousser, laisser échapper.

V.

vacant, vide, vacant.
vain, vain, vaniteux ; *in vain,* en vain ; *he speaks in vain,* (may be turned) il a beau parler.
valuable, précieux, de grande valeur.
value, valeur, f., prix, m.
varied, varié, divers.
variety, variété, f.
various, divers, différent.
vasistas, m.
vehicle, voiture, f., véhicule, m.

venerate, vénérer ; *(venerated) by,* de.
veneration, vénération, f.
Venice, Venise, f.
versatility, universalité, f., (not *versatilité*).
verse, vers, m.; *in verse,* en vers.
very, très, bien, fort ; *very much,* beaucoup, extrêmement ; *to the very...,* jusqu'au...
vessel, vase, m.; (ship) vaisseau, m., bâtiment, m.; *sailing vessel,* navire (bâtiment) à voiles, m.
vexation, humeur, f., dépit, m., chagrin, m.
vicar, (Anglican) ministre, pasteur.
viceroy, vice-roi, m.
Victoria, Queen, la reine Victoria.
victorious, victorieux, conquérant.
victory, victoire, f.
view, vue, f. ; *to expose to view,* mettre en vue, en évidence.
vigor, vigueur, f., puissance, f.
village, village, m.
villager, villageois.
villain, scélérat, misérable.
vine, vigne, f.
vinegar, vinaigre, m.
vineyard, vignoble, m., vigne, f.
violate, violer.
violence, violence, f.
violent, violent ; (passionate) emporté, violent.
virtuous, vertueux.
viscount, vicomte ; *how does the viscount get on?* est-ce que (monsieur) le vicomte fait des progrès ?
visible, visible.
vision, vision, f.
visionary, visionnaire, chimérique.
visit, n., visite, f.; *to pay a visit to,* faire une visité à.
visit, v., visiter, faire (rendre) visite à ; (of an explorer) toucher à.
visitor, visiteur, m.
vizier, vizir, visir.

VOCABULARY. 169

voice, voix, f.; *I had no voice*, je ne trouval pas de voix.
volume, volume, m., tome, m. (The binding distinguishes the "volume," while the "tome" marks the divisions made by the author. Hence a "volume" may contain several "tomes." However, volumes are often numbered as "tome I., II., etc."
Vosges, f. pl.; *Vosges Mountains*, les Vosges, la chaîne des Vosges.
vow, vœu, m.; *made a vow that*, fit vœu que (de with infin.)
voyage, voyage (par mer), m.; *voyage of discovery*, voyage de découvertes.

W.

wainscot, lambris, m., boiserie, f.
wait, attendre; *to wait for*, attendre; *waiting for the return of*, en attendant le retour de; *to wait for it to come*, attendre qu'il vienne.
waiter, garçon.
waiting-room, salle d'attente, f., (omnibus station) bureau, m.
waken, v. a., éveiller, réveiller; v. n., s'éveiller, se réveiller; p. 50, sortir de sa torpeur.
Wales, le Pays de Galles; *Prince of Wales*, Prince de Galles.
walk, n., marche, f., promenade, f., tour, m., (of a horse) pas, m.; *at a walk*, au pas.
walk, v., marcher, aller à pied; se promener; *he walked out*, il sortit; *to walk up and down*, se promener (marcher) de long en large; *to walk (horses)*, faire aller au pas, remettre au pas; *walking along (F. street)*, en passant par....; *to walk away*, s'en aller, s'éloigner.
wall, mur, m., muraille, f.
wandering, errant.
want, n., manque, m., défaut, m., (destitution) misère, f.; *for want of*, faute de.
want, v., avoir besoin de, manquer de; *to be wanting*, manquer; (desire) vouloir, désirer; *I don't want any*, je n'en veux pas; *you don't want people to know*, vous ne voulez pas qu'on sache; *how do you want the pockets?*, comment voulez-vous les poches? *I want two more*, il me faut encore deux; *there was a nail wanting in one of*, il manquait un clou à l'un de.
war, guerre, f., (*fell*) *in war*, pendant la guerre; *great in war*, grand dans la guerre; *to make war on*, faire la guerre à.
Seven Years' War, guerre de sept ans, f.
warble, gazouiller.
warm, chaud; *he is warm*, il a chaud; *it is warm (weather)*, il fait chaud.
warn, avertir, prévenir.
warrior, guerrier, m.
war-ship, vaisseau (navire) de guerre, m.
wash, laver, (linen) blanchir.
wasp, guêpe, f.
waste, n., désert, m.; *barren waste*, terre inculte, f., terre (terrain) vague.
waste, v., gaspiller, gâter, dissiper.
watch, n., montre, f.
watch, v. a., regarder (attentivement); *to watch that...*, veiller à ce que...
watch-guard, chaîne de sûreté, f.
watch-maker, horloger.
water, n., eau, f.
water, v., abreuver (un cheval, etc.); arroser (un pays, la terre, etc.)
waver, vaciller, balancer, flotter.
wax, n., cire, f.
wax, v., cirer.
way, chemin, m., route, f., voie, f., manière, f., façon, f., moyen, m.; *on the way*, en route, chemin faisant; *on its way to*, en route pour; *to give out on the way*, rester en route; *to lose one's way*, s'égarer; *to make one's way towards*, se diriger vers; *the best way is to*, le mieux est de; *in this way*, de cette manière (façon), comme ça; *this way*, (direction), par ici; *that way*, par là; *that's the way I...*, c'est comme cela que je..., voilà comme etc.; *by way of*, par (la) voie de.

weak, faible.
weakness, faiblesse, f.; (foible) faible, m.
wealth, richesse(s) f., biens, m.
wear, porter.
weary, las, fatigué; *to grow weary*, se lasser, s'ennuyer, se dégoûter.
weather, temps, m.; *the weather was hot*, il faisait très (bien) chaud.
weave, (fabric) tisser; (fig.) tramer, ourdir; *to weave his plots*, ourdir la trame de ses pièces.
week, semaine, f., huit jours, m.
weep, pleurer; *to weep for*, pleurer, v.a.
weigh, v.a., peser; *to weigh anchor*, lever l'ancre; v.n., peser.
weight, poids, m.
well, n., puits, m., source, f., fontaine, f.
well, adv., bien, eh bien!, (health) bien (portant), guéri, rétabli; *I am well*, je me porte bien; *to live well*, faire bonne chère; *to be well up in (a subject)*, être (très) fort en (sur), être ferré (à glace) sur; *to be well-to-do*, être, vivre à son aise; *as well as*, aussi bien que, en même temps que, (often simply) et aussi.
well-equipped, supérieurement (bien) monté.
well-known, bien connu, célèbre, renommé.
west, n., ouest, m.; adj., ouest, de l'ouest, occidental.
western, (de l') ouest, occidental.
wet, mouillé, *to get wet*, se faire mouiller.
whalebone, baleine, f.; *with the whalebones coming out*, dont les baleines sortaient.
what, interrog. adj. and pron. quel(s), quelle(s); quoi, que, (exclam.) quoi!; (indirect interrog.) ce qui, ce que, (see p. 2, note 1.); *what for*, pourquoi, pour quoi faire; *what shall I do?*, que voulez-vous que je fasse?; *what is he?* que fait-il? quel est son état

(sa profession)?; *what is that?* qu'est que (c'est que) cela? comment?
what, rel. pron., ce qui, ce que; *what is more*, qui plus est.
whatever, quelconque; *whatever may be...* quel que soit...
wheat, blé, m., froment, m.; *wheat culture*, la culture du blé, f.
wheel, roue, f.
wheel-barrow, brouette, f.
when, quand, lorsque, où, que; *on the evening when*, le soir où; *one day when*, un jour que.
whenever, quand, toutes les fois que, chaque fois que.
where, où, là ou.
whereupon, sur quoi.
whether, si; *whether...or*, si...ou, soit...soit.
which, qui, que, lequel; (interrog.) lequel, quel; (beginning a clause, and without a definite antecedent) ce qui; *on which*, (beginning a clause) sur quoi; *to which*, (beginning a clause) à quoi; *from which*, duquel, etc., d'où, dont; *of which*, duquel, etc., dont; *in which*, dans lequel, etc., où.
whiffle-tree, whipple-tree, palonnier, m.
while, whilst, conj., (during the time that) pendant que, tandis que; (while, on the other hand) tandis que; *while in Paris*, trans., while they were in Paris.
while, n., temps, m.; *it is not worth the while*, il ne (en) vaut pas la peine, ce n'est pas la peine.
whip, n., fouet, m.; (horse-whip for riding) cravache, f.
whip, v., fouetter.
whisper, chuchotement; *in a whisper*, tout bas.
who, qui; *whom*, que; (interrog. or obj. of prep.) qui; *whom you will only have to command*, à qui tu n'auras qu'à commander.
whole, entier, tout; *a whole hour and a quarter*, d'une bonne heure et quart; *during the whole year*, de toute l'année.

why, pourquoi, que ; (exclamation) mais, eh bien, comment ; *why so?*, pourquoi donc ?

wicked, méchant.

wide, large, étendu, grand ; for idioms of dimension, see "long"; *to open wide,* ouvrir tout(e) grand(e).

width, largeur, f.

wife, femme, épouse.

wig, perruque, f.

wild, sauvage, farouche.

will, vouloir ; *will* as mere sign of future is not separately translated, and sometimes not even when expressing unemphatic volition, especially when in the contracted form *'ll* ; *if you would do,* si vous vouliez bien faire.

William, Guillaume.

willingly, volontiers, de bon cœur ; *very willingly,* de tout mon cœur.

win, gagner, remporter ; mériter ; *to win (an advantage) over,* remporter...sur ; *to win some one over,* gagner, convaincre qn.

wind, vent, m.

winding, tortueux, sinueux.

window, fenêtre, f., croisée, f.; *out of the window,* par la fenêtre.

wine, vin, m. ; *wine district,* pays vignoble.

wine-merchant, (wholesale) négociant en vins ; (wine and spirit vendor) marchand de vin.

wing, aile, f.

winged, ailé.

winter, n., hiver, m. ; adj. d'hiver ; *in (the) winter,* en hiver.

wipe, essuyer.

wire, fil de métal, m., fil de fer ; ...*wire,* fil de...

wise, sage.

wisdom, sagesse, f.

wish, vouloir, désirer ; souhaiter ; *I wished very much to,* j'avais bien envie de ; *to wish one a good day, etc.,* souhaiter le bonjour (le bonsoir, la bonne année) à qn.

wit, esprit, m.; (pers.) bel esprit.

witchcraft, sorcellerie, f.

with, avec, à, de ; (means) par, moyennant ; *with a swollen face,* le visage gonflé ; *(with his) hat in (his) hand,* le chapeau à la main; *with (in) a...voice,* d'une voix...; *mouth with long teeth,* bouche à longues dents ; *with which I bought,* contre lequel j'ai acheté.

without, prep., sans.

witness, témoin, m., (testimony) témoignage, m.; *to bear witness to,* témoigner de, rendre témoignage de.

witticism, jeu d'esprit, m., bon mot, m.

witty, spirituel.

wolf, loup, -ve.

woman, femme.

wonder, n., étonnement, m.; merveille, f.; *(it is) no wonder...,* ce n'est pas étonnant...

wonder, v., s'étonner ; *I wonder whether, what, how, when,* je me demande si, quel, comment, quand.

wonderful, merveilleux, étonnant, remarquable, extraordinaire.

wonderfully, merveilleusement ; *wonderfully well,* p. 54, il fait des progrès étonnants.

wood, bois, m., forêt, f.

wool, laine, f.

woollen, de laine ; *woollen goods,* lainerie, f., lainages, m. pl.

word, mot, m.; parole, f. ; *in a word,* en un mot ; *in these words,* en ces termes ; *a man of few words,* un homme qui parle peu, parlant peu ; *upon my word,* sur ma parole (d'honneur), parbleu !

work, n., travail, m., ouvrage, m. ; (book, work of art) ouvrage, (but see p. 13, note 2.); (collected works) œuvres, f. pl.; *to go to work,* se mettre à l'ouvrage ; *cabinet work,* ébénisterie, f.; *work of art,* œuvre d'art.

work, v., travailler ; (ferment) fermenter, s'agiter.

work-woman, ouvrière.

world, monde, m., terre, f.; *in the world,* dans le monde, au monde ; *the greatest in the world,* le plus grand du monde ; so also on p. 74, *of the world ; not for the world,* pour rien au monde, jamais de la vie.

worm, ver, m.

worse, adj., plus mauvais, pire; (in health) plus mal; (wicked) plus méchant; adv., plus mal, pis; *worse murdered,* plus abominablement échorché.

worship in, assister à l'office à.

worst, le plus mavais, (blot) la plus grande.

worth, be, valoir, (see also under "while")

worthless, sans valeur, sans mérite; *is worthless,* ne vaut rien.

worthy, digne, (*of, to*=de).

would, when not the mark of the conditional, is rendered by the tenses of *vouloir,* (see "will.")

would-be, prétendu, soi-disant, en expectative.

wound, blesser.

wrap, rouler, envelopper.

wretch, misérable.

wretched, (unhappy) malheureux, misérable; (bad) misérable, vil, mauvais.

write, écrire.

writer, écrivain, auteur.

writing, écriture, f., (book) écrit, m., ouvrage, m.

wrong, mal, m., tort, m.; *tort* is said of the one who *does* the wrong and not, as in English, of him who suffers it; hence, *I am wrong, I am in the wrong,* j'ai tort: *he wrongs me,* il me fait tort: *the wrongs he has done,* ses torts; *I have done wrong sometimes,* j'ai fait du mal quelquefois.

Y.

yard, the corresponding word in France is *mètre,* m., =one and one tenth of a yard (89·371 inches); the Canadian word is *verge,* f.

year, an, m., année, f.; *for many years,* pendant bien des années: *New Year's Day,* le jour de l'an; *in the year 1895,* l'an 1895, en 1895.

yes, oui; (in reply to a negative assertion) si, si fait.

yesterday, hier; *yesterday evening,* hier (au) soir.

yet, adv., encore, toujours; *not yet,* pas encore; conj., pourtant, toutefois, cependant.

yield, se rendre, céder, fléchir, consentir.

yonder, là, là-bas.

you, vous, tu.

young, jeune; *young men,* jeunes gens.

your, votre, vos; ta, tes.

yourself, vous (-même), toi (-même).

youth, jeunesse, f., minorité, f.

Z.

zeal, zèle, m.; *showed great zeal,* déploya un zèle ardent.

zealot, zélateur, -trice; enthousiaste.

INDEX TO EXERCISES.

Abernethy and his patient	54
Æsop and the ass	21
America, The man who knew	1
Anarchism, Remedy for	19
Arab's disappointment, The	11
Arc, Joan of	78
Artist and his master, The	23
Ass beaten by the horse, The	28
Ass, The disobliging	66
Beaumarchais and the nobleman	11
Beecher's horse-shoeing	50
Bishop and the commercial traveller, The	55
Blind man's candle, The	3
Bohemian and the trousers, The	25
Bossuet	81
Boy and the magistrate, The	26
Boy frightened by the ass, The	59
Canadian discoveries, Early	16
Canadian forest trees	113
Canadian missionaries, Early	91
Carriage, The parts of a	107
Cartier, Jacques	88
Catherine, The Empress, and the snow-drop	43
Champlain, Samuel de	89
Charlemagne	72
Charles XII. and his secretary	1

INDEX TO EXERCISES.

Chartier, Alain, and the Queen	58
Chesterfield, Lord, and his funeral	30
Clerk, The polyglot	24
Clovis, the first king of France	71
Complet, Passengers for	111
Concierge and his door, The	29
Conundrum	26
Crébillon's reverie	47
Denis and Dives	34
Diamond, The stolen	9
Domenichino at work	47
Edinburgh, The Duke of	51
Facino Cane and the stolen cloak	40
Fairy godmother, The	60
Falconet and his patient	27
Fly and the bull, The	32
Fly and the coach, The	36
Foote and the young man	23
France, Eight cities of	101
France, The geography of	97
France, The products of	98
France, The trees of	99
Franklin and the stranger	44
Frederick the Great and his corporal	39
Frederick the Great and the deserter	6
Frederick the Great and the snuff-box	7
French-Canadian farmer, The	111
French murdered	29
Frontenac, Count de	90
Fox's revenge, The	42
Garrick in Paris	49
George III. and the wine-merchant	43
Gray's dread of fire	42

Harness, Parts of the	107
Henry IV. and the peasant	15
Henry IV., Sketch of	74
Henry VIII. and Sir Thomas More	40
How to get rich	61
How to keep dry	33
Hugo, Victor	79
Irish gentleman's ingenious steward, The	30
Irish gentleman's message, The	29
Irishman's watch, The	31
Irishman and the wounded soldier, The	38
Irish sailor, The	25
Jena students	35
Johnson, Dr., and his relations	27
Johnson, Dr., in Scotland	31
Joseph, The Emperor, incognito in Paris	46
Joseph, The Emperor, and the landlady	41
Judge and the turkey, The	64
Labor and Capital in the United States	20
La Fontaine and madame de la Sablière	2
La Fontaine and the apple	45
Lawyer, The diminutive	33
Lefebvre, Marshal, and his old comrade	65
Le Sage and the duchess	14
Longfellow and the child	48
Louis IX.	73
Louis XIV. and the Count de Guiche	10
Louis XIV. and the old officer	2
Louis XIV., The reign of	75
Lunatic's explanation, The	25
Madeleine of Verchères	93
Malherbe and the Archbishop of Rouen	29
Malherbe and the Abbé Desportes	35

Marivaux and the beggar	4
Miller, Joe, and Cross	52
Millet's *Angelus*	63
Miser and the cheese, The	69
Molière	80
Montaigne	81
Mouse, The young, and her mother	68
Napoleon I.	76
Nash, Beau, and his prescription	28
Nightingale and the glowworm, The	57
Obstinacy, Extreme	8
Octogenarian and the young men, The	39
Ogre and his enemy, The	34
Orleans, The Duke of, and the petitioner	56
Parmenon's pig	12
Paris	100
Parisian house, The	103
Parisian omnibus and tram-car, The	108
Pascal	85
Pocket-book, The king of Prussia's	13
Priest, The scalded	8
Priest and the thief, The	4
Professor's ride, The German	48
Quack and his pills, The	23
Quebec, The first Bishop of	94
Queen and the countrywoman, The	64
Rabelais	83
Raphael and the cardinals	30
Retz, Cardinal de, and Ménage	5
Rights of Man, The true	22
Roquelaure and the Auvergnat	7

INDEX TO EXERCISES.

Rossini's dinner.. 82

Sailor and the teapot, The 41
St. Lawrence, The 17
Saxon and his cheese, The 61
Secret of happiness, The 51
Servant, The confidential 26
Sheridan and Cumberland 36
Slanderer, The sponging 24
Somerset, The Duke of, and Seymour 53
Sorbonne, The 95
Sympathy with both sides 5

Tennyson and Houghton 49
Tom and the horse-shoe 66
Toper and his bed, The.. 28
Toto's New Year compliments .. 26
Turenne 58

Utopia, Missionaries for 46

Valois, The dynasty of the.. 18
Vestris, Madame, and the comedian 23
Vicar and the farmer, The.. 32
Villager and the pumpkin, The .. 62
Viscount's tutor, The 54
Vivier and the concierge.. 25
Vizier, The shrewd 55
Voltaire 86

Want of a nail, For 56
Wasp and the bee, The 67
Wife, The diminutive 24
Wolf about to die, The 37
Wolf and the fox, The.. 37
Worse, How it might have been 27

www.ingramcontent.com/pod-product-compliance
Lightning Source LLC
Chambersburg PA
CBHW020247170426
43202CB00008B/267